# WHY DOES
# BRIGHT
# LIGHT
# MAKE YOU
# SNEEZE?

# WHY DOES BRIGHT LIGHT MAKE YOU SNEEZE?

### Over 150 Curious Questions & Intriguing Answers

Andrew Thompson

## Ulysses Press

Published in the U.S. by
ULYSSES PRESS
P.O. Box 3440
Berkeley, CA 94703
www.ulyssespress.com

ISBN: 978-1-61243-799-6
Library of Congress Control Number 2018930782

Printed in Canada by Marquis Book Printing
10 9 8 7 6 5 4 3 2 1

Managing editor: Claire Chun
Editor: Renee Rutledge
Proofreader: Shayna Keyles
Layout: Caety Klingman
Front cover design: what!design @ whatweb.com
Artwork credits: see page 247

Distributed by Publishers Group West

*To Lucy, Hugo, and Felix*

# Contents

# ❓ WHAT MAKES GRUMPY OLD MEN GRUMPY?

We've all seen him many times, with the scowling face, the shaking head, the aggressive tone—the grumpy old man. What is he grumpy about? Anything and everything: the government, the economy, the state of the sidewalk, teenagers, the chirping birds. But why? Were Jack

Lemmon and Walter Matthau acting in *Grumpy Old Men*, or is that just how they are?

Also known as *grumpy old man complex* or *irritable male syndrome*, the crankiness of many older gentlemen can be attributed to a number of factors.

Psychology plays a major role. By the age of 60 or 70, many men have retired from work or are approaching retirement. A feeling of worthlessness can result, like that of being thrown on the scrap heap, with daunting thoughts of a future sitting around the home with no aspirations left to attain. As friends and loved ones die, men can become aware of their own mortality and health problems, resulting in depression and anxiety. Men tend to suppress these concerns, leaving them prone to anger and outbursts directed toward other people or situations, for whatever trivial reason.

In addition to emotional changes, changes in an old man's brain are the main root of the condition. As men age, testosterone levels fall, usually significantly by age 60. By 70, they tend to be at half the level of a young man, indicating a kind of male menopause. A decrease in testosterone typically leads to fatigue, depression, and a reduction in libido and powers of concentration. This often leads to irritability and an inability to deal with the nuances of everyday life. The result? A grumpy old man.

But it's not just men. Irritable male syndrome has been noticed in the animal kingdom with red deer, reindeer, sheep, and Indian elephants. During breeding, when testosterone levels are high, these males are confident and competent. However, as the mating season ends and their testosterone drops, they become nervous and agitated, often striking out irrationally.

In addition to a drop in testosterone in older men, another key change takes place. They lose brain tissue in the frontal lobe region at almost three times the rate of women. The frontal lobes are involved in motor function, memory, problem solving, concentration, reasoning, and impulse control.

So, the next time an old man goes berserk at you for stepping foot on his lawn, remember that he's not pretending to be Clint Eastwood out of *Gran Torino*. There's a physiological reason for his behavior, and it's not all his fault. Try to wave, smile, and blame biology.

## WHY DO PEOPLE'S EYES TURN RED IN PHOTOS?

Known as the *red-eye effect*, it is very common for people's pupils to appear bright red in photographs, particularly when those photos were taken at night or in low light. But what causes us to look like possessed nocturnal creatures?

When a camera uses a flash that is very close to the lens (like in most compact cameras), the light from the flash can sometimes travel into a person's eye, through the cornea and pupil, and to the retina (a layer of light-detecting cells) at the back of the eye. The retina then reflects the light back through the pupil, and the camera records it.

One of the functions of the pupil is to control the amount of light that enters the eye, but the reason the flash travels into the eye is because it occurs too quickly for the pupil to close in time. The pupil doesn't have time to constrict, so the light enters the eye and reflects out as red. But why red? That's because of the rich blood supply of the choroid, a layer of tissue at the back of the eye that nourishes the retina. The blood-red color of the retina absorbs some of the light, reflecting the rest back in red.

So, who gets affected the most?

The amount of red light that reflects back through the pupil depends on the level of melanin in the layers behind the retina. Melanin absorbs some of the light, so fair-skinned people with blue eyes, who have less melanin, will generally exhibit a greater red-eye effect than people with brown eyes. Children also usually have a more pronounced red-eye effect because their pupils enlarge more in low light. This allows more light to enter and escape, accentuating the red-eye effect.

To reduce the red-eye effect, you can try a number of techniques. Don't look directly at the camera so the light from the flash won't enter your eyes as easily; brighten the room so that your eyes are less dilated; move the flash and the lens farther apart, which will only work with cameras that have an external flash that can be disconnected; and, wait for it—don't get drunk. The slow reaction times of people who are drunk also affects their eyes. Alcohol tends to dilate the pupils, which then don't constrict as quickly as in sober people. This means that more light from the flash is able to enter the eye and reflect back out.

## ❓ WHY ARE MOST PEOPLE RIGHT-HANDED?

While other primates don't generally show a preference for right- or left-handedness, around 90 percent of humans are right-handed. This is one of the traits that separates us from our animal cousins.

A number of hypotheses explain this predominance, but most aren't backed by any significant evidence. Some say left-handedness results from prenatal exposure to certain hormones (one being a synthetic estrogen-based fertility drug) or the ultrasounds some mothers receive during pregnancy that could allegedly alter the brains of unborn children. It is commonly believed that most people are right-handed because of social and cultural influences, such as mothers and teachers forcing children to use their right hand for writing, or children using their right hands to conform.

However, the reason most of us prefer our right hand is because we actually evolved that way.

Scientists have examined the jawbone and teeth fossils of one of our earliest ancestors, *Homo habilis* (literally, the *handy man*), who lived in Tanzania, Africa, around 1.8 million years ago. The markings and wear on these teeth fossils show striations slanting to the right. This indicates that material was held in the mouth with the left hand, while the right hand held a stone tool to strike the material, or to bring food to the mouth, occasionally hitting the teeth and leaving marks. Marks left in this fashion are widespread among the fossil records and are believed to be a strong indicator of right-handedness.

But why did our ancestors evolve to be right-handed in the first place?

The human brain is comprised of two halves: The left hemisphere deals with language and motor skills, and the right hemisphere deals with vision and spatial awareness. The left hemisphere controls the right side of the body and vice versa. The main theory as to why most people are right-handed is the division of labor within the brain. Language and fine motor skills, such as detailed tool building, are controlled by the left side, leaving the right side of the brain to deal with vision, and enabling our ancestors to better detect threats in the form of predators. Then, as the language abilities of our ancestors improved, the left hemisphere of the brain developed even further, intensifying its motor skills ability. This translated to a predominance in right-handedness.

But while we as a race have evolved to be mainly right-handed, the next time you're watching ball sports, have a look at the number of lefties who play. It's often greater than 10 percent. In tennis, for example, a number of the greats have been left-handed: Rod Laver, John McEnroe, Jimmy Connors, and Rafael Nadal, just to name a few. So, while left-handed people are sometimes the object of derision and are scorned with names like *cack-handed*, perhaps the average left-hander is actually more coordinated than the rest of us.

## ❓ WHY DO DOGS HAVE WET NOSES?

The dog—man's best friend. A loyal companion and protector for thousands of years. They come in a variety of shapes and sizes, but they all have a wet nose. Why? There's a biblical explanation. When God flooded the world and all the animals collected on Noah's ark, two dogs patrolled the vessel, keeping an eye on things. One day the dogs noticed a hole in the side of the ark, which water was gushing through. One dog ran for help while the other stuck his nose in the hole to plug the leak. By the time Noah arrived to repair the hole, the dog was gasping for breath but had prevented a major disaster. As a badge of honor for this heroic deed, God bestowed on all dogs a cold and wet nose.

Here are some other explanations for the dog's wet nose:

Their noses secrete a thin layer of mucus, which allows them to absorb scent chemicals from the air, greatly enhancing their sense of smell. Added to this is the fact that dogs frequently lick their noses. Apart from doing this as a cleaning mechanism, they are also licking off the scent chemicals and presenting them to the olfactory glands on the roof of their mouths. This aids in their sense of smell.

A dog's wet nose also helps cool it down. Dogs sweat by secreting moisture from their paws and nose. The wet nose is a way of releasing heat after exertion and helps to regulate the dog's body temperature.

Dogs also commonly sniff around outside, sticking their noses into wet grass or bowls of water. This adds to the wetness on the nose.

But if you asked the wolf from *Little Red Riding Hood*, he'd give you this reason: "All the better to smell you with, my dear."

## ARE COMPUTER GAMES AS ADDICTIVE AS COCAINE?

"It could be a lot worse, they could be into drugs." Comments such as this are common when parents describe the habits of their teenage children, one of which is playing computer games. The problem is that many experts liken gaming to drug use.

Dr. Peter Whybrow, the director of neuroscience at UCLA, calls video games "electronic cocaine," while they are known by some experts in China as "digital heroin." Dr. Nicholas Kardaras, the executive director of the rehab clinic The Dunes East Hampton, said in 2016, "I have found it easier to treat heroin and crystal meth addicts than lost-in-the-matrix video gamers or Facebook-dependent social media addicts."

But are computer games actually addictive, causing real changes in the brain, the way drugs such as cocaine do? Yes, but only to a degree.

Dopamine is a neurotransmitter in the brain that increases when we experience something pleasurable. In our ancestors, it served as an important survival benefit, rewarding a successful or beneficial behavior that promoted well-being, such as finding a meal or a mate.

Scientists have found that when computer games are played, particularly ones with progressing levels of challenge, dopamine is released as a reward response to achievement. The dopamine signals to the brain that it has succeeded in the challenge, and this prompts the brain to want to repeat the action to receive more pleasure in the form of dopamine. As each new level of the game poses a greater challenge, even more dopamine will be released when it is successfully negotiated. A 1998 study by a team of scientists in London, England, led by Professor Matthias Koepp, found that the dopamine levels in subjects playing video games increased 100 percent.

Drug use produces a similar response in the brain, and the euphoric effect from cocaine is the direct result of an increase in dopamine. Cocaine elevates dopamine in the brain to such a high level that as the drug wears off and the dopamine is reduced, the person seeks to restore it by taking more cocaine. This can result in an addiction, the same way a computer game can become addictive.

But are the levels of dopamine production and addiction potential the same for computer games and cocaine? No. To put it into perspective, here is a list of activities and the amount dopamine increases for each:

- Eating food—100 percent
- Playing computer games—100 percent
- Having sex—200 percent
- Taking cocaine—350 percent
- Taking methamphetamine—1,200 percent

To answer the question, yes, playing computer games increases dopamine levels and can be addictive, but to a far lesser extent than taking drugs. So, don't worry if your teenage children are playing the odd computer game—just make sure they're not eating and having sex at the same time, as that could definitely lead to a serious addiction.

## ❔ WHY IS THE EAGLE A RECOGNIZED SYMBOL OF THE UNITED STATES?

The bald eagle is the national bird of the United States. This iconic bird appears on a number of official US government seals, including the presidential seal, the presidential flag, coins, and the United States passport. Why?

Soon after the Declaration of Independence was signed on July 4, 1776, the Continental Congress asked Thomas Jefferson, Benjamin Franklin, and John Adams to design an official seal for the new nation. However, these men failed to come up with a design that met Congress's approval. When the work of two later committees also failed to fulfill the task, Charles Thomson, the secretary of Congress, was given the job in 1782. Thomson chose what he considered the best elements of the designs that had been submitted.

Utilizing a design by Pennsylvanian lawyer William Barton, which was introduced by the third committee and included a small, white eagle, Thomson enlarged the bird and replaced it with a bald eagle. The final design, which Congress adopted on June 20, 1782, was that of a bald eagle holding a bunch of arrows in one talon and an olive branch in the other. A shield of red and white stripes covered the breast of the bird, with a crest over the eagle's head and a cluster of thirteen stars surrounded by rays emanating to a ring of clouds. A banner was placed in the beak of the eagle, bearing the words *E pluribus unum*—"Out of many, one."

The bald eagle was officially adopted as the emblem of the United States five years later, in 1787.

The eagle had been used as a symbol of governmental power and strength since Roman times, and it is thought that the founders of the United States were fond of comparing their new nation to the Roman Republic. President John F. Kennedy summed up the attributes of the bird in 1961 when he wrote to the Audubon Society: "The founding fathers made an appropriate choice when they selected the bald eagle as the emblem of the nation. The fierce beauty and proud independence of this great bird aptly symbolizes the strength and freedom of America."

Contrary to popular legend, there is no evidence that Benjamin Franklin ever publicly opposed the choice of the eagle and preferred the wild turkey. Privately, though, this is another matter. In a 1784 letter to his daughter he wrote: "I wish the bald eagle had not been chosen the representative of our country. He is a bird of bad moral character."

Mind you, given the other choices that were available, such as the crow or the chicken, the bald eagle must have seemed the more regal choice.

## ❓ WHY DO PEOPLE SAY "CHEESE" WHEN BEING PHOTOGRAPHED?

"Say cheese!" is the simple instruction issued by photographers to elicit a smile from those being photographed, regardless of their age. It has become so commonplace that the word *say* is often omitted from the command, and most subjects don't even respond. They just know to smile at that point. But how did this bizarre directive come about?

Etymologists are unsure as to who coined the phrase, or if there is any link between the expression and the word *cheese*. It is generally thought that it was probably coined impromptu by a photographer, but nobody knows who or when. The word is useful for this purpose because the "ch" sound causes a person to open the lips while the "ee" sound pushes the cheeks outward, draws back the lips, and bares the teeth in a pose that resembles a smile.

The earliest recorded references to the saying are from the 1940s, when the phrase was popularized. In particular, the article "Need to Put on a Smile? Here's How: Say 'Cheese,'" from an October 1943 edition of the Texas newspaper *The Big Spring Daily Herald*, made this comment: "Now here's something worth knowing. It's a formula for smiling when you have your picture taken. It comes from former Ambassador Joseph E. Davies and is guaranteed to make you look pleasant no matter what you're thinking. Mr. Davies disclosed the formula while having his own picture taken on the set of *Mission to Moscow*. It's simple. Just say 'cheese,' it's an automatic smile. 'I learned that from a politician,' Mr. Davies chuckled."

It is thought that the politician referenced in the article was Franklin D. Roosevelt, who Davies served under, so we may well owe "say cheese" to none other than FDR. Whatever its origins, it was certainly an improvement on what was used in the late 19th century. At that time, a small, tightly shut mouth was considered beautiful, so there was a different, less jovial expression that was said to obtain the desired face: "Say prunes."

# WHY DO OCEANS AND NOT LAKES HAVE TIDES?

A tide is the rise and fall of the sea, which can be seen moving up and down a beach. But we never see the same effect on the shore of a lake. Given that lakes are a body of water, don't they have tides as well?

They do, we just can't see them.

Tides are caused by the gravitational pull of large celestial bodies, mainly the sun and the moon. On the side of the earth that faces the sun and the moon, the water from the ocean is pulled forward to create a high tide. On the opposite side of the earth, away from the sun and the moon, the water drains away to compensate for the high tide. This creates a low tide. The tides' heights differ the most during the new and full moons, because the moon and sun are aligned, making the gravitational pull stronger.

In lakes, the same forces are at work, but on a much smaller scale. They experience the same gravitational pull as oceans, but because they are much smaller than oceans, their tides are also smaller and are difficult to detect. The bigger the body of water, the bigger the pulling effect and the bigger the tide.

While all bodies of water are affected, it takes an ocean for the effects of gravity to be very noticeable. Even the Mediterranean Sea isn't large enough for significant tides. And Lake Michigan, which is nearly 500 miles long, has a tidal range of only a few inches. Any other movement of water up and down the shore is as a result of wind, or waves from watercraft. Smaller lakes do register tidal effects as well, but they are generally imperceptible. Even your bathtub has tides, but don't worry, the water isn't about to overflow just yet—we're talking about a tidal range of only a few atoms.

## WHY DO PEOPLE RUB THEIR EYES WHEN THEY'RE TIRED?

We've all seen young children clench a fist, rub it vigorously into their eye, then start yawning. There's no surer sign that it's time for bed, but why the eye rubbing?

Here are a few physiological reasons for this behavior:

1. As a person gets tired, the eyes get fatigued as well. By rubbing the eyes, eyelids, and muscles around the eyes, the soreness and tension are relieved. It's similar to rubbing a sore arm muscle after playing sports.

2. Tired eyes are dry eyes. Having been exposed to air for a long period of time, the lubricating film that bathes the front of the eyes in a protective layer begins to evaporate. Rubbing the eyes stimulates the lacrimal glands, which then produce more fluid to bring moisture to the eyes and provide some relief.

3. There's a connection between the muscles that move the eyes and the heart. Applying pressure to the eyes stimulates the vagus nerve, which causes a reflex that actually slows down the heart rate and relaxes you. This can make you even more tired.

So, the next time your toddlers rub their eyes, it's time for bed, despite whatever protests or excuses might be made.

# WHY IS THERE A BLACK DOT IN AN OTHERWISE WHITE BIRD DROPPING?

Is there anything more annoying than when you're walking around town, well-dressed and away from home, and *splat!*, you get hit? You look down at your clothes, expecting the worst, and there it is. Bird shit—the bane of statues, cars, and hapless pedestrians throughout the entire world. As you try to wipe the white goo away, you notice a small black dot in its midst and wonder why it's there.

Birds possess a cloaca, an all-purpose orifice that, as well as being the place for reproductive entry and egg laying, provides a single exit point for the intestinal and urinary tracts, which expel waste simultaneously. In layman's terms, birds piss and shit at the same time.

But why the black dot?

The kidneys of birds extract nitrogenous waste from their bloodstream, but instead of releasing it as urea dissolved in urine, like many other animals do, birds excrete it in the form of uric acid. Uric acid has a low solubility in water, which means it can be expelled with minimal water loss. As a result, it emerges as a white, paste-like substance. This paste is effectively urine. The black dot is fecal matter from the intestinal tract. Because the two are expelled at the same time from the same opening, but from two different systems, they have little time to blend, so the black fecal matter sticks in the middle of the viscous white acid.

So, the next time you have the unsavory misfortune of being struck by a bird relieving itself in flight, at least you'll be armed with the knowledge that you've technically been hit twice—two birds with one stone, so to speak.

## WHAT IS THE DIFFERENCE BETWEEN A BISON AND A BUFFALO?

*Bison (top) and buffalo (bottom)*

If you take a drive around Yellowstone National Park, you will hear many tourists refer to the vast herds of buffalo in the area. The bovine herds are actually bison, so why do so many people mistake them?

It's easy to understand why some people confuse the buffalo and the bison. Both are large, horned bovines. The confusion probably arose because the early American settlers referred to the bison as buffalo due to their similarity in appearance. But it's actually easy to distinguish the two animals, especially if you focus on the four Hs: home, hump, horns, and hair.

1. **Home.** There are actually two types of bison: the American bison and the European bison. The latter consists of a small population in remote parts of Poland, but the bison that we know well live only in North America. There are two types of buffalo as well, but neither of them are in America, nor have they ever

been. The water buffalo is indigenous to South Asia, while the Cape buffalo is from Africa.

2. **Hump.** Another key difference between the two animals is the bison's hump. Bison have a large hump at the shoulders and a massive head, while buffalo don't have these characteristics. The large hump and head allow the bison to plow away drifts of snow.

3. **Horns.** Buffalo have very large horns, up to 6 feet in length with pronounced arcs, while the horns of bison are far shorter and sharper, nestled in close to the head.

4. **Hair.** Owing to their freezing winter habitat, bison have thick fur, as well as a dense beard. Buffalo are beardless and have only a light covering of fur. Bison are also brown in color, while buffalo are closer to black.

Despite these significant differences between the two animals, perhaps the real reason Americans still call their native bovines *buffalo* is because otherwise, the legend of William Cody would have to be changed to "Bison Bill," and that just doesn't sound as good.

## HOW DID THE THUMBS-UP GESTURE COME TO MEAN OK?

There is no more universally recognized hand gesture than the thumbs-up. Achieved by closing the fist and extending the thumb upward, it signifies approval and means that everything is OK. Despite how common it is, the origins of the gesture are not certain, and a number of theories have been proposed.

1. **Opposable thumbs.** Carleton S. Coon, in his 1954 book *The Story of Man*, suggested that the gesture came about in early man because he had opposable thumbs. Coon claimed this after observing Barbary apes in Gibraltar using the thumbs-up. He concluded that any species who possesses such thumbs would be likely to adopt the gesture. Dissenters of this theory believe that the apes were merely imitating people.

2. **Business transactions.** In his 1979 book *Gestures: Their Origins and Distribution*, Desmond Morris claimed that the gesture was used in medieval times as a method of sealing a business transaction. Once all the terms were agreed, the thumbs-up was given, indicating that a deal had been made.

3. **Archery.** Another theory is that it comes from archers in medieval England, who needed to signal that their bow was in order and they were ready to fight. The fistmele (a term used to describe the correct distance

between the bow and the strings) was about the length of a fist with the thumb extended, and archers would use that gesture to check it before signaling with the same gesture that everything was OK.

4. **Ancient Rome.** A common theory is that the Latin phrase *pollice verso*, meaning thumbs-down, was used in gladiatorial contests to describe a hand gesture made by the crowd of spectators when passing judgment on a defeated gladiator. A man who had fought well and received a majority of thumbs-up would be spared, while a majority of thumbs-down condemned him to death. The 1872 painting "Pollice Verso" by the French artist Jean-Léon Gérôme depicts such a scene.

5. **World War II.** During World War II, the thumbs-up gesture was used extensively by American pilots to signal the ground crew that they were ready to fly. It has been suggested that the gesture was brought back from China by the Flying Tiger Brigade of American pilots based there during the war. The Chinese at the time used the gesture to mean *number one*.

It may be that the thumbs-up gesture arose independently in a number of these ways, but it declined in popularity in the United States from the end of World War II until 1974, when it made an incredible resurgence. That was the year the television show *Happy Days* began, and it was Fonzie's usage of the gesture with both hands, accompanied by "aaaaaay," that brought the expression to mainstream America.

## ❓ WHY DOESN'T ALUMINUM FOIL GET HOT IN THE OVEN?

You pull a baking tray covered in aluminum foil out of a 400°F oven. The baking tray is far too hot to touch, the food on it is sizzling and you need to take it off with a fork, but when you touch the foil, it isn't the slightest bit hot. How is this possible?

There are two reasons: specific heat capacity and surface area.

Aluminum has a very low specific heat capacity. This means it only takes a small amount of energy to heat it up. Additionally, aluminum foil is extremely thin, with little mass. This means it is unable to store much heat, and whatever heat it does have is quickly lost through its large surface area. (If the same sheet of thin foil is rolled tightly into a ball and put into the oven, it will remain hot after it's removed for far longer because it has a much smaller surface area from which to lose heat.)

Once heated, it only has to release a small amount of energy to cool down. And because it can't store much thermal energy in the first place, when that energy is released onto your hand, not much heat is transferred.

In addition, human tissue has a high heat capacity, which means that it takes a lot of heat to raise its temperature. The heat from the aluminum is absorbed by the fingers, but

it does not raise the temperature in your fingers enough for you to feel it.

While the aluminum foil doesn't heat up to the extent that food does and it cools down very quickly, the baking tray and the food have more mass compared with surface area, so they can hold more heat and take much longer to lose it.

## WHY DO WOMEN DANCE MORE THAN MEN?

If you go to any place where there's a dance floor, you will notice a lot more women dancing than men. Women dance with men when they can, but seem equally happy to dance alone or in groups of women. Men, on the other hand, are usually very reluctant to strut their stuff, and often only do so under duress. Is there a reason for this marked disparity between the sexes?

Women dance for pure pleasure. They often see dancing as a form of self-expression and not as a talent show, not caring about what other people think of their style. Men, on the hand, usually derive very little joy from the mere act of dancing and only want to dance if they can dance well. They often feel they are being judged on their style, so think they should either dance like an expert, or not dance at all.

These different mindsets exist for a reason. As is often the case, evolution provides the most plausible explanation.

Scientists believe that early man danced to bond and communicate as part of a courtship display. To dance well requires good health, coordination, rhythm, stamina, and strength. Skillful dancing indicates genetic fitness and the ability to produce and provide for better offspring. This quality would have likely made someone more attractive to the opposite sex and given them an evolutionary advantage.

As with most species in the animal kingdom, our ancestral females, limited by the number of offspring they could have, sought quality over quantity. Dancing was one key way to determine the best mate. This would have led women to dance more in an attempt to entice the men to dance so they could see what the men were made of. Dancing up close would have also given the women an opportunity to garner further information from the men, including pheromones, to assess whether they were a good match.

Our ancestral male pursued the female, seeking quantity over quality so as to increase the chances of propagating his genes. The need to impress the female gave him a fear of dancing, because he knew he had to dance well or risk being shunned. There was a lot to lose, so only men who were very good dancers would have taken the risk. Women, on the other hand, were being pursued, so they had nothing to lose if they danced badly, and everything to gain by using it as a tool to obtain information about a potential suitor.

Because of this early social dynamic, most women evolved to love dancing, while most men evolved to hate it. And you only need to look at any dance floor in America to realize the truth behind this hypothesis; it was surely a man who wrote the Scissor Sisters song "I Don't Feel Like Dancing."

# ❓ DO VEGETARIANS LIVE LONGER?

Only a couple of decades ago, many people had not even met a vegetarian, but the number of Americans who are turning away from meat is rising steadily. There are a variety of reasons for this increase, including animal welfare and ethical concerns, religious beliefs, and, of course, health considerations. But does this popular new way of life actually make people live longer?

Much research over the years has linked eating red meat with a number of health risks, including cardiovascular disease, stroke, diabetes, and certain cancers. Vegetarianism has been found to reduce these risks. One 2013 study that followed 96,000 Seventh-Day Adventists (whose religion advocates a vegetarian diet) in the United States from 2002 to 2007 found that vegetarians had a 12 percent lower risk of death from all causes than meat-eaters did, and in fact, lived an average of six to nine years longer.

In 2012, a team led by T. Huang of Zhejiang University in Hangzhou, China, conducted a meta-analysis, which combined the data from multiple studies on vegetarianism. The team concluded that vegetarians had a 29 percent lower risk of early death from heart disease, and an 18 percent lower cancer risk.

But is it all as simple as that? Many experts say it's not and claim that the statistics are skewed. On average, vegetarians are health-conscious people. They are less likely to smoke, drink alcohol, or be overweight, and more likely to exercise and be married. These are all factors that tend to contribute to a longer life, suggesting that factors other than an abstinence from meat may be the reason vegetarians live longer.

A 2003 article, "Mortality in British Vegetarians," written by a group led by Tim Key of the University of Oxford's Cancer Epidemiology Unit, drew similar conclusions, stating: "British vegetarians have low mortality compared with the general population. Their death rates are similar to those of comparable non-vegetarians, suggesting that much of this benefit may be attributed to non-dietary lifestyle factors such as a low prevalence of smoking and a generally high socio-economic status, or to aspects of the diet other than the avoidance of meat and fish."

While there is still some debate on the topic, it seems that while vegetarians do generally live longer, their avoidance of meat is not the reason. And until the issue is resolved definitively, why live with regret and resist that big, juicy steak? As 103-year-old English vegetarian Roy Hobbs said in 2015, "It wasn't worth it."

## WHY DO MIGRATING BIRDS BOTHER FLYING BACK NORTH?

It is a well-known phenomenon that many species of birds migrate south for the winter. That perilous journey expends a great deal of energy and comes with many associated risks. A lot of birds perish along the way, which begs the question, once they've safely arrived in the south, why do they bother flying back north at all?

Birds migrate south for a number of reasons. The winter in the north of America can be a tough environment for birds. As snow and frost take hold, food becomes more difficult to find, and simply keeping warm takes a lot of energy. Many birds migrate south to warmer climates where resources are more abundant.

But while life for birds during winter is undoubtedly more salubrious in the south, it does have its drawbacks. The northern migrants are forced to compete with large numbers of birds that live in the south year-round. This means that food and nesting locations are hotly contested. The warmer climates of the south also tend to be home to many more parasites and infectious diseases that the northern birds are forced to combat.

Because of these negative aspects, once spring arrives, the migrating birds leave the south and fly back home to the

north, where things are far better. As spring takes hold in the north, plants begin to bud again and insect populations burgeon. An abundance of food, as well as nesting locations, are available. These resources enable the birds to live well and raise their own healthy young. During the summer, the length of each day is also much longer in the north than in the south. This affords the birds more hours of daylight in which to gather food and feed their young. In order to flourish, the birds must fly back north once the winter is over.

It's a bit like people from New England going on vacation to Florida. It's great to be down there in the sun for a break, but it's always nice to get back home.

## ❓ WHY DOES TIME FLY WHEN YOU'RE HAVING FUN?

It's such a common complaint—you sit at work completely bored all day and the minutes seem like hours, yet when you go on vacation it seems to pass in the blink of an eye. "Time flies when you're having fun," people often say, but is there any science to this phenomenon?

Psychologists believe that people do perceive time differently depending on their mental state and what they are doing. When people are bored and uninterested, their minds tend to wander. When this happens, people usually look at the time very regularly to see how much longer it will be until they can do something they enjoy. Conversely, when people are busily engaged in an enjoyable activity, their minds are focused and they don't look at the time as often. The more often you look at the time, the slower it seems to pass, and vice versa. These findings were recorded in a 2003 study by Dinah Avni-Babad and Ilana Ritov, "Routine and the Perception of Time," published in the *Journal of Experimental Psychology: General*.

Paradoxically, though time flies while you're having fun, your memory perception of that time is usually the opposite. When you think back on an interesting passage of time, it generally involves a lot of new experiences or memorable moments. You are able to retrieve many of those moments from your memory, so in retrospect, it feels as if the time lasted a lot longer. On the other hand, long, boring days when you did nothing, which felt like an eternity at the time, will feel like they flew by when you remember them, as they added very little new information to your memory. Perhaps the mark of a successful life, then, is that while the days flew by, the years felt long and interesting.

While time definitely does fly when you're having fun, there's another factor to consider, according to psychologists Alan Kingstone and Anthony Chaston from the University of Alberta. They conducted a study where participants were asked to look for a given object in a certain time frame. Because of the time pressure they were under, the subjects reported that time had seemed to pass very quickly. This same experience is often reported by students who are under time pressure during an exam, or people working at a hectic job where they struggle to complete their required tasks.

Given that stressful, time-pressured activities such as taking an exam are not usually considered "fun" by most people, perhaps the expression should really be "time flies when you're attentively engaged and focused in any activity, whether you derive pleasure from it or not." Not quite as catchy as the original, is it?

## WHY DOESN'T RAIN COME DOWN A CHIMNEY, WHEN SMOKE CAN GET OUT?

It makes logical sense that if smoke can get out of a chimney, then rain should be able to get in to the fireplace, potentially extinguishing the fire. Why doesn't this happen?

It does get in, to a degree, although a number of protective layers help combat this apparent anomaly.

1. A lot of chimneys have a chimney cap, which is a flat piece of metal that is held above the chimney by legs,

forming a sort of umbrella. There is enough room between the top of the chimney and the cap to let smoke out, but not enough room to let much rain in.

2. The tops of chimneys are usually fairly small, and rain rarely falls straight down, more likely falling at an angle because of wind. The small target means that not a lot of raindrops enter the chimney.

3. Most chimneys have a bend in them, which is why you can't see out from the bottom. The main reason for this arching rear wall is to create what is called a smoke shelf. Any rain that comes down the chimney will accumulate on this shelf.

4. There is a damper in most chimneys that slides open or shut to regulate the smoke flow. When the chimney is not in use, it is usually closed so that any rain that enters the chimney will pool on the damper, where it will have time to evaporate.

5. Any rain that gets in the chimney is likely to hit the walls and get soaked up by any soot that has built up there. This excess water would also likely evaporate fairly quickly.

6. Finally, the small quantity of rain that manages to successfully negotiate this obstacle course and make it down into the fireplace simply remains unobserved.

## WHAT MAKES A WHIP CRACK?

Whip cracking is the act of producing a sharp cracking sound through the use of a leather whip. Commonly used from horseback to assist in moving livestock in the American West, it is also a competitive sport in Australia.

For a whip to crack, a portion of it must move faster than the speed of sound to create a sonic boom. The sonic boom of the whip is created by shock waves that generate enough energy to make an explosive sound. Since 1905, scientists suspected it was the sonic boom that was responsible for the cracking sound, but it wasn't until 1958 that this was confirmed when some high-speed photography that had been taken in 1927 was analyzed.

The commonly held belief is that the tip of the whip breaks the sound barrier and creates the sonic boom, or crack. However, in 2002, Alain Goriely of the University of Arizona conducted a study that concluded "the crack of a whip comes from a loop traveling along the whip, gaining speed until it reaches the speed of sound."

Regardless of whether it's the tip of the whip or a loop on the whip that causes the crack, how does it travel at such high speeds? A whip begins with a wide diameter that tapers to a much thinner diameter. Using the arm, the whip cracker imparts energy to the beginning of the whip, and as the energy travels down the tapering whip, it is amplified exponentially, making the loop traveling down the whip move exponentially faster. When the whip, whether the loop or the tip, reaches the speed of sound, a sonic boom is created and the whip cracks.

So, how long has whip cracking been around in America? About 150 million years, give or take. Paleontologists believe that the first whip crack was done by a large lizard-like dinosaur that lived in North America in the late Jurassic period. That animal wasn't herding cattle with a stockwhip, but rather had a long, tapering tail that resembled a whip. It is thought that the reptile was capable of cracking its tail and producing a sonic boom comparable to the sound of a canon.

And just how fast does a whip (or dinosaur tail) have to travel in order to crack? The speed of sound is 767 miles per hour, so faster than that. Given that the typical passenger jet travels at around 570 mph, that's pretty fast.

## WHY DO RABBITS WIGGLE THEIR NOSES?

One of the key mannerisms of the rabbit is the nose wiggle. They are constantly wiggling and twitching their noses back and forth in a very noticeable way. Why?

1. **Breathing.** On a basic level, wiggling the nose expands the nasal orifices and allows the rabbit to inhale more air.

2. **Smelling.** More significantly, the nose wiggling enhances the rabbit's sense of smell, allowing it to better detect danger, food, and potential mates. When a rabbit wiggles its nose, sebaceous glands located on the mucous membranes are activated, creating moisture.

Their sense of smell is increased by the wet surface, which collects scents from the air. The nose twitching also moves about the olfactory detection areas in the nose, exposing them to more air and allowing the rabbit to smell better.

3. **Cooling.** Rabbits only perspire a small amount through the pads of their feet, so in order to cool down, they lose heat from their long ears and expel hot air through their nose. In an attempt to cool down, the rabbit's respiratory rate increases markedly when they're hot, and this increases the movement of their nostrils.

4. **Emotional.** When a rabbit is relaxed, its nose will usually remain quite still. However, when a rabbit is stressed or nervous, its pulse and respiratory rate increase, and its nose wiggling increases in response. Similarly, if a rabbit is excited or interested in something, like when it's about to feed or it sees a potential mate, its nose will wiggle more than usual.

There may, of course, be another key reason that rabbits wiggle their noses—maybe they're just trying to look cute.

# WHAT ARE HYENAS LAUGHING AT?

When most people think of hyenas, they think of packs of scavengers who giggle and laugh maniacally at each other. Do these African hunters have a warped sense of humor, or are they laughing for a completely different reason?

Hyenas produce a variety of noises. To rally a group against lions they make a deep sound called lowing, which is similar to the mooing of a cow. They make deep, staccato sounds called alarm rumbles to signal danger, and when a mother hyena calls her infants out of a den, she makes a groaning sound. But it is the strange laughing noise for which the hyena is most famous.

 It is only the spotted hyena that emits the laugh, but it's not actually a laugh at all. These giggling noises are used to signal frustration when they are fighting for food, or when they are in some kind of social conflict.

Hyenas live in a complex matriarchal structure where competition for food is intense and social status is crucial. The females are dominant, and there is a strict hierarchy, especially when feeding. A 2009 study led by Nicolas Mathevon at the University of California, Berkeley, found that a hyena's characteristic laugh carries critical information about the animal's age and status in the group. The researchers found that the more subordinate animals laugh more than the dominant ones, which led them to conclude that it is done out of frustration. In an attempt to get their share of the food, the younger hyenas will laugh and giggle. They will also do this if they manage to secure a piece of meat and other hyenas are chasing them. It is a signal for the pursuers to back off, but it is done in angst. The hyenas will also laugh when they are all feeding on a carcass, as they bite and nip at each other as a means of ensuring the complex group dynamic is maintained.

And it's not just their laugh that is misunderstood. Hyenas scavenge less than a third of their food and are in fact the most prolific predator in Africa. They are an intelligent animal, with a sophisticated social structure. Perhaps they're laughing at us, because we've read them all wrong.

## ❓ WHY DO DELIVERY TRUCK DRIVERS KEEP THEIR ENGINES IDLING WHEN DROPPING SOMETHING OFF?

How many times do you see a delivery truck stop at the curb and the driver jump out with his parcel, leaving the truck still running? Why do they do this? Doesn't it use a lot more fuel, and wouldn't it be better to turn off the engine like everybody else does? Not necessarily, and here are some reasons why:

1. Continually stopping and starting an engine creates significant wear and tear. An engine runs better if it is kept warm, rather than letting it cool down. This is particularly so in cold environments, where starting a cold engine can be difficult.

2. Cold conditions are not good for batteries. If a truck is kept warm, the batteries remain charged and there is no risk of not being able to restart the truck if the batteries are marginal.

3. Keeping a truck warm keeps the oil in the transmission and axles effective. When a truck cools down, the oil can get heavy, slowing down the gears until it warms up.

4. The comfort of the driver is a key factor. In cold conditions, the cabin will remain warm with the heater

running, and in hot conditions, the air conditioning will keep it cool. Driver comfort is generally considered one of the major reasons that engines are left running.

5. Most delivery trucks run on diesel, and an idling diesel engine uses very little fuel. It can actually be better for emissions as well, because a plume of smoke is often forced out of the exhaust every time a truck is started.

6. Laziness is probably the most common explanation that the rest of us provide, and there is some basis for it. If the driver is picking up and dropping off parcels all day, and they'll only be out of the truck for a minute, why not just leave it running to save the hassle?

## ❓ WHY DO SHORT MEN TEND TO HAVE HIGHER VOICES THAN TALL MEN?

After winning the Kentucky Derby on an imposing 1,200-pound thoroughbred and collecting over $1 million for the owner, the successful jockey is jubilant. Raising his arms in the air, the diminutive jockey gets up to make his acceptance speech and sounds like Mickey Mouse on helium. This is almost always the case with racehorse jockeys and other short men. It can't be a coincidence, so why is this the case?

The depth of the human voice is related to a few physical factors: the vocal cords, the lungs, and the chest cavity.

The vocal cords are stretched horizontally across the larynx. When air is brought up from the lungs to make speech, they vibrate. The length, size, and tension of the vocal cords determine the pitch of the voice. The longer and thicker the vocal cords, the deeper the voice. It's similar

to guitar strings: A shorter and thinner string produces a higher-pitched sound, compared to a long and thick string. Men have longer and thicker vocal cords than women and children, and shorter men tend to have shorter cords than taller men. This is because taller men are larger than shorter men generally—they have longer arms, longer legs, a longer neck, and longer vocal cords. This means that the average short man will have a higher voice than the average tall man.

Tall men also usually have bigger lungs and a larger chest and abdominal area than short men. This additional space allows the voice to resonate more, adding to the depth of voice. The opposite effect occurs with short men, with the voice not having as much room to echo deeply.

So common is the difference in voice between tall and short men that people can often gauge how tall someone is simply by listening to their voice. In a 2013 study led by psychologist John Morton of Washington University in St. Louis, twenty-four volunteers listened to the recorded voices of different pairs of people and were then asked to say who was taller. They were also asked to rank a group of five people according to their heights, based solely on their voices. The participants were able to distinguish the taller of the two speakers nearly 63 percent of the time, significantly better than if they were picking randomly, and they were also able to order the groups of five with far better than random accuracy.

## HOW DO BLIND PEOPLE DREAM?

Everyone dreams, some more vividly than others, but a key element of most dreams is the visual aspect. It's often like watching a movie with a weird plotline. But if blind people can't see and don't know what it's like to see, do they dream, and if so, how?

People's dreams are based on the things they have experienced in their lives. Blind people do dream, and how they dream depends on how much they've ever been able to see.

If a person goes completely blind after about the age of five, their dreams will still contain visual experiences that are similar to those who can see. As time passes, the pictures in their dreams will usually become more blurry, with the prevalence of experiences from other senses, such as sounds, increasing. A person who had diminished vision in early life will usually have dreams with diminished visual experiences, similar to what they used to see.

People who have been totally blind from birth or before the age of five will usually only have auditory dreams. These are dreams that contain sounds and no images, just like what they experience when they're awake. Their dreams are just like the dreams of people who can see, only without the pictures. Blind people also report an increase of taste, smell, and touch sensations in their dreams, which compensate for the lack of visual imagery.

A 2014 Danish study published in *Sleep Medicine* assessed the dreams of a number of people with different levels of sight, from blind to full sighted. All the people who could see reported visual imagery in their dreams, while none of the people who were blind from birth did. For the people who had become blind later in life, the longer they had lived without sight, the less they saw in their dreams. However, a far greater percentage of the blind people compared with the people who could see reported tasting, smelling, and touching sensations in their dreams. The dreams of all participants were otherwise similar in nature, with social interactions, successes, and failures. The notable difference was the number of nightmares, with the blind people having around 25 percent, compared with 6 percent by people who could see. The researchers speculated that this was related to the evolutionary theory about why nightmares exist—as a means of preparing the mind to adapt to and cope with the threats of life. This theory is consistent with the blind people's nightmares, which included getting lost, being hit by cars, losing their guide dog, or falling over, all of which are genuine fears in their everyday lives.

# WHY DON'T CATS LIKE TO SWIM?

While most cats are curious about water and will carefully stick a paw in, when it comes to taking the plunge, they are more than reluctant. As many a cat owner will tell you, any attempt to bathe a cat is done at your own peril, often resulting in painful claw marks. Given that cats are such clean animals, constantly preening themselves, why do they hate water so much?

1. **Independence.** Cats like to experience life on their own terms and tend to be intolerant of change. They don't like surprises and generally approach new things with a great deal of circumspection. Because most cats are not used to swimming, they do not take kindly to

the concept being thrust upon them in the form of a bath.

2. **Sensitive.** Cats can smell the chemicals in tap water and pools far more acutely than we can, so they are reluctant to want to bathe or swim.

3. **Heaviness.** When a cat's coat gets completely wet, it gets heavy. This makes the cat feel slow and less able to maneuver. Cats do not like being in a situation that they can't easily escape from, so the feeling of being in water, or drenched by it, is a frightening one.

4. **Cold.** Cats maintain a higher body temperature than humans, making it harder for them to get and stay warm. A cat's coat does not shed water easily, so once a cat is wet, it is difficult for them to get dry and warm again.

5. **Evolution.** Most domestic cats are descended from cats that lived in dry, arid regions, such as Arabia, where bodies of water to swim in were not prevalent. These cats were not accustomed to swimming, because there was no evolutionary need for it, and as a result, an aversion to water is a trait that has been passed down to modern cats.

Mind you, not all cats hate water. The Turkish Van, a breed of cats that lives near the shore of Lake Van in Eastern Turkey, loves to swim. Their mothers rear them to dive in as kittens, and they'll actually swim out to meet fishing boats in the hope of getting a free meal. Most Turkish Van cats these days, however, live as pets in England, where it is too cold to swim and their fish comes from a can.

# WHY ARE THE BUTTONS ON MEN'S AND WOMEN'S SHIRTS ON DIFFERENT SIDES?

The buttons on men's and women's shirts look similar when they're done up, but they're actually on different sides—men's on the right and women's on the left. It seems a completely pointless difference, but is there a genuine theory to explain it?

One theory is that it was because men held their sword in their right hand and the position of the buttons made it easier to unbutton a shirt or coat while holding their weapon. This, however, does not explain why women's buttons are on the opposite side.

Another popular theory is that women's clothing was designed so that they were forced to fasten the buttons using their weaker left hand as a reminder that they were inferior to men. There is no basis for this proposition.

The likely origin of this practice dates back to Victorian England. Women of the upper class at the time were keen to demonstrate the wealth of their families. As a means of showing this, they would dress in expensive and elaborate clothing, with multiple layers. Buttons were costly and only the rich could afford them, so  as a status symbol, the best dresses had many. Dressing in these intricate outfits was a time-consuming task, so upper-class women also had ladies' maids, who dressed them. As a result, it became customary to make women's clothes that were slightly easier for other people to button. Given that most people were right-handed, the buttons were affixed on the left because the ladies' maid would be facing them.

The rich men, on the other hand, did not wear such complicated garments, and while they had valets, most men tended to dress themselves. Because of this, the buttons were placed on the right, designed for the fact that most men were right-handed.

When sewing machines were invented and buttoned clothing started being mass produced and became cheaper, the less privileged people wanted to emulate the fashions set by the wealthy, so the buttons remained where they had been, men's on the right and women's on the left.

It's a quirk that has just never been changed, and it doesn't make much difference today—unless you're a cross-dresser, that is. In that case, it's beneficial to be ambidextrous.

## WHY ARE THERE DENTS ON THE TOP OF COWBOY HATS?

No one item is more closely linked to the American West than the cowboy hat. While there are a number of styles, the cowboy hat is typically a wide-brimmed, high-crowned hat worn and prized by the men who work the land. There is also always a dent on the top of the hat, which, at first blush, appears to serve no purpose. Why is it there?

There is no definitive answer to that question, although it is thought that it started by way of accident and continued by way of fashion. Originally, the hats didn't have dents, but they developed through wear. When the cowboys in the days of yore donned and doffed their hats, they would grab the crown of the hat in a three-fingered manner, pushing dents into the hat, one on either side and one in the top. This was done as a matter of practicality as it allowed the hat to be grasped more easily. Over time, these three dents became permanent.

The hat was a key possession of the cowboy, and a very worn-looking hat that contained dents and creases was full of character. It indicated that a man had done a lot of time in the West, that he was an old hand, full of experience. As a result, it became the fashion to have  these marks on the cowboy hat, and soon the cowboys were intentionally creating them.

In time, the particular style of dent on the top of the hat was used to help cowboys identify with certain subcultures and groups. The top dent served another purpose too, helping to protect the cowboy from the weather by sluicing rain away from the face. As the denting trend became universal, commercial hatmakers included them in the hats, and they persist to this day.

So, which style of dent is the best? There are a lot to choose from. There's the Cattleman, the Carlsbad, the Rodeo, the Bullrider, the Quarter Horse, and the Tycoon, just to name a few. It all depends on the look you're going for and which group you want to feel a part of.

## WHY DO ONLY OLD MEN HAVE HAIRY EARS?

Hair is not the friend of the aging man. While the hair on his scalp thins and falls out, it springs up in new places, like the shoulders, back, nose, and ears. But why do formerly bare ears suddenly become hirsute?

Vellus hair is short, thin, barely noticeable hair that covers most of a person's body during childhood. As people age, some of the vellus hair changes. During and after puberty, this hair can transform into thicker, darker hair known as terminal hair. This happens to a greater extent in men than in women, and by the time some men are old, the soft and downy vellus hair on and in their ears would have become closer to what you'd expect to see on a werewolf.

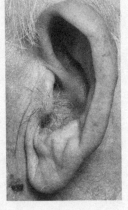

The cause of this transformation isn't fully understood.

The leading theory to explain the hairy ears is prolonged exposure to testosterone. While the testosterone levels in old men usually drop, it is thought that the hormone may have a cumulative effect, so that as a man ages, the hair follicles are exposed to a greater overall amount of testosterone, and this encourages the growth of long black hairs.

Scientists also believe that the hairy ears of older men could be related to the fact that they go bald on their heads. Male pattern balding is caused by an enzyme called 5-alpha reductase, which converts testosterone into dihydrotestosterone (DHT). DHT acts by binding to receptor sites on the cells of the hair follicles to cause specific changes. On the head, these changes inhibit hair growth, while on the ears, they enhance it. The result—long, black, coarse ear hair. Supporting this theory is the fact that women rarely go bald, and they rarely have bushy ear hair either.

Whichever theory is correct, most experts agree that testosterone is responsible in some way for the hairy ears of old men. So, while most men want a lot of testosterone to make them manly, there's certainly a balance to be struck. Too much can make men appear a little more manly than they might like.

## WHY DOES LOOKING AT THE SUN MAKE SOME PEOPLE SNEEZE?

Have you ever stepped out of a dim subway station into the bright sunshine, felt a tickle in your nose, and then suddenly sneezed? If you have, it's likely you've experienced the photic sneeze reflex, a condition that affects somewhere between 18 and 35 percent of the population in the United States. But just what causes this bizarre phenomenon?

Colloquially known as sun sneezing, it was noticed as far back as Ancient Greece, when the philosopher Aristotle wrote in his book, *Problems*: "Why does the heat of the sun provoke sneezing, and not the heat of the fire?" While the exact mechanism is not fully understood, it is not the heat of the sun, but its brightness, that causes the sneeze.

A reflex typically associated with an irritation in the nose, sneezing can't generally be controlled. When the nerve endings in the mucous membrane in the nose become irritated, the brain receives a message to sneeze in order to expel the irritant from the nose. But if there is no specific irritation in the nose, as is the case when looking at the sun, what causes the photic sneeze reflex?

One theory is that it is caused by parasympathetic generalization, a process that occurs when one part of the nervous system, such as the pupil of the eye, is stimulated, activating other parts of the system as well, such as the membranes in the nose.

A more supported hypothesis is also nervous system–related. First proposed in 1964 by Henry Everett, a psychiatrist at Johns Hopkins University Hospital in Baltimore, the photic sneeze  reflex is said to be caused by a confusion of nerve signals in pathways very close to each other. The trigeminal nerve is a complex nerve with three major branches leading to the eyes, nose, and jaw. It is this nerve that detects a tickling in the nose and alerts the brain to effect a sneeze. When bright light enters the eyes, however, it is the optic nerve that sends signals to the brain to constrict the pupils. The pathways involved in these two reflexes are close, but do not usually interact. But with sun sneezers, it is thought that the optic nerve pathway stimulates the trigeminal nerve pathway. This means that exposure to bright light sends a signal to the brain to constrict the pupils, but because of the mixed pathways, a signal is mistakenly sent to the nose as well.

While scientists have not yet identified the specific genes responsible for sun sneezing, it is known to be an inherited trait.

Many experts agree that sun sneezing is a harmless quirk, but there is evidence to suggest that it could interfere with the vision of pilots, or motorists emerging from a dark tunnel. And the benefits? None, although one dubious theory is that it's a legacy from our cavemen forefathers, who, after sleeping in dark and dusty caves, would emerge into the sunlight and sneeze, expelling any unwanted dust from their noses as they did.

## ❓ WHY DO PEOPLE BECOME EMOTIONAL WHEN DRUNK?

Drinking alcohol affects our personalities in a number of ways. Some people become happy drunks, while others want to fight. But at one time or another, we've all been an emotional drunk, crying into a drink in the middle of a crowded bar. Why does this embarrassing behavior happen?

Alcohol impacts every organ and system in the body, but its effect on the brain is what determines our behavior. After getting absorbed into the bloodstream through the stomach lining, it then circulates through the body and reaches the brain. There, it acts as a depressant, interrupting and slowing the normal flow of neurotransmitters, the electric signals between the synapses. In essence, the central nervous system is slowed, and we experience a loss of motor function, a delay in reaction time, and a lowering of inhibitions. As we consume more drinks, more areas of the brain are impacted, including the limbic system, a set of structures under the cerebrum. The limbic system is believed to be the emotional center of the brain, controlling our behavior and keeping our emotions in check. Once it's affected by alcohol, we become subject to mood swings and exaggerated mental states.

But why the crying? As a general rule, drunken emotions are just exaggerated versions of our sober personalities. A happy person will become giggly and silly, and an angry person will become aggressive. And if you're feeling sad or nostalgic before you start drinking, there's a good chance you might end up crying.

There is some good news though. The limbic system is also responsible for helping to form memories, so if you do become a bumbling mess, you most likely won't remember it the next day anyway.

## ❓ WHY ARE GRAVES DUG 6 FEET DEEP?

Look no further than the drama series *Six Feet Under* to realize just how commonplace the concept of graves being dug to that depth is. Is there a reason for it, and how did it originate?

The idea of graves being 6 feet deep began in 1665 with the outbreak of the plague in England. As the Black Death swept the country, the Mayor of London laid down various laws as a measure to contain the disease and prevent further infections. These laws were specified in the document,

*Orders Conceived and Published by the Lord Mayor and Aldermen of the City of London, Concerning the Infection of the Plague.* Under the heading "Burial of the Dead," it was stated that "all the graves shall be at least 6 feet deep."

Following the plague, graves continued to be dug to 6 feet for a number of practical reasons. Apart from preventing the spread of disease, that depth was thought to be enough to stop animals from smelling and digging up a body. It was also considered a sufficient depth to keep a body safe from exposure resulting from soil erosion. Six feet was also thought to be deep enough to hinder grave robbing, which became a lucrative business in the 1800s, when stolen cadavers were sold for medical research.

The required depth of graves in modern times varies considerably, even from state to state. Many states require a minimum of 18 inches of soil on top of the casket. If the body is not enclosed, 2 feet of soil is often mandated. In reality, however, most modern graves are probably around 6 feet deep anyway.

## IS IT POSSIBLE TO EAT FIFTY EGGS LIKE IN COOL HAND LUKE?

If you've ever seen the famous 1967 movie *Cool Hand Luke,* you'll remember the scene where Paul Newman's title character claims he can eat fifty hard-boiled eggs. "Nobody can eat fifty eggs," says one of the inmates. The inmates then bet all their money against Luke eating the eggs within one hour without throwing up. Luke manages to pull off

the feat, which has led to many discussions over the years as to whether it's actually possible.

It is possible, although there are a number of obstacles. Fifty hard-boiled eggs weigh about 6 pounds and occupy about 3 liters of stomach space. The average human stomach holds 1.5 liters, but the stomach does stretch, which would allow it to hold the fifty eggs.

You would need to produce a lot of saliva to be able to swallow the eggs, which are of a dry texture. Failing that, which is highly likely, you would need to drink a lot of water during the process.

The combined eggs would contain approximately 3,850 calories, so you would feel extremely full, making the later eggs more difficult to eat.

If you did manage to get all fifty down, they would likely remain in your stomach for a number of hours before being broken down enough to reach your large intestine. There they would sit for up to three days while the body's bacteria fed on the proteins to produce various gases, including hydrogen sulfide, which just happens to smell like rotten eggs. So, if you do this in a jailhouse like *Cool Hand Luke* did, spare a thought for your cellmate.

It all sounds like a rather superhuman effort, but if Joey "Jaws" Chestnut were reading this, he'd be smirking at the thought of such a light snack. Chestnut is a competitive eater and holds the world record for eating hard-boiled eggs—a mere 141 in eight minutes.

# WHY ARE BASEBALL DUGOUTS BELOW GROUND LEVEL?

Like the name suggests, the baseball dugout is an area that is slightly depressed below field level. It's the area where the coaches and players who are not currently participating in the game sit. But why is it not at the same level as the field?

1. The main reason is to offer the spectators a better view of the game. If the waiting players were at field level, they would obstruct the crowd, who wouldn't be able to properly see the home plate, which is a key area where most of the action takes place. Being underground also provides more room for the spectators to sit, allowing stadiums to have a greater number of premium field-level seats.

2. Dugouts create a barrier between the players and the fans. When the players were at ground level, very close to the spectators, it was easy for the fans to distract or insult the players, or even throw things at them. The dugout gives the players protection from this.

3. Similarly, dugouts protect the players from being hit by foul balls. Being slightly underground allows the players to duck down easily to avoid a flying ball.

4. The dugout protects the players from the weather. With walls and a roof, the players can avoid sitting in the sun or the rain.

Despite these benefits, dugouts are primarily underground at professional baseball games. At most amateur ballparks, where locating them below field level would be cost prohibitive, the players sit on benches or on the grass. Nevertheless, the term *dugout* is still used in these circumstances.

## ❓ WHY DOES GARLIC CAUSE BAD BREATH?

Picture the scene: You're about to meet someone for a first date and you grab a quick snack on the way. It tastes good and hits the spot, but a few minutes later, there's a distinct taste in your mouth. No! Surely it didn't have garlic in it. You breathe onto your hand in an attempt to smell your breath. It did contain garlic. There is no worse a social faux pas. But why is garlic usually the culprit when it comes to bad breath?

Garlic contains a sulfuric compound called allyl methyl sulfide (AMS). It is very similar to the compounds that are produced by the anaerobic bacteria that cause non-garlic bad breath. There are two ways that AMS makes your breath smell bad:

1. When you eat garlic, the compounds will get in your mouth and immediately give you garlic breath. They also promote the growth of some microbes already in the mouth that cause bad breath, which exacerbates the problem. These compounds and microbes will remain in the mouth until they are flossed and brushed out.

2. AMS is a gas that is absorbed into the blood during the metabolism of garlic. From the blood it is transferred to the lungs, where it is then exhaled as garlic breath. In a 1936 study conducted at Cincinnati General Hospital, two doctors fed garlic soup to a patient with cancer of the esophagus. Because of the cancer, the soup was fed through a tube that entered directly into the stomach. Despite the soup never being in the patient's mouth, he still had garlic breath three hours later.

Because the garlic is in your bloodstream and is exhaled in your breath, there is very little you can do to get rid of it except wait until it has passed through your body. Thorough tooth brushing will only do so much. There are a number of suggested remedies; however, their effectiveness is debatable.

- **Parsley.** This can help neutralize the odors of garlic, which is why a lot of recipes that use garlic also use parsley. Try chewing on parsley after eating garlic.
- **Lemon.** Lemon has antibacterial properties that can help neutralize the garlic odor. Washing your hands in lemon juice will also remove the smell from your hands.
- **Tea.** Drinking green or mint tea, which contain polyphenols, can reduce the sulfuric compounds that garlic produces.
- **Milk.** Drinking milk may also help, because the fat it contains helps to neutralize the odor.

The bad (or even worse) news about garlic breath? It's not just the breath. The odor-producing compounds that are absorbed into the bloodstream are also exuded from your pores. So, it's not just bad breath, it's bad body. It's little wonder that wearing garlic around the neck or hanging it in windows was used to ward off evil spirits. They might be evil, but even they don't want to stink.

## ❓ DO CATS ALWAYS LAND ON THEIR FEET?

On the rare occasion that you see a cat lose its balance and fall, it will invariably perform an acrobatic twist in the air before landing on its feet unscathed. How do they manage such an incredible feat, and do they always land on their feet?

The technique, known as the cat righting reflex, is the cat's innate ability to orient itself as it falls so that it lands on its feet. Most cats perfect the reflex by six weeks of age.

French scientist Étienne-Jules Marey first recorded the reflex in 1890, by dropping a cat and using a camera to capture its fall. He later watched in slow motion to determine how the cat managed to land on its feet.

Marey determined that a vestibular apparatus in the cat's inner ear acts as its orientation compass so that it knows which way is up. Once this is determined, it rotates its head to see where to land. Then the cat's unique skeletal structure comes into play. Cats don't have a collarbone, and they have an unusually flexible backbone with thirty vertebrae, as opposed to the twenty-four in humans. This gives the cat added mobility, allowing it to arch its back as it positions its front feet underneath its body, with the front paws close to the face to protect it from impact.

The minimum height for the righting reflex to be effective is about 12 inches. Any higher than that and they will almost always land on their feet. But height is a factor in whether a cat lands without injury. When a cat lands, the leg joints

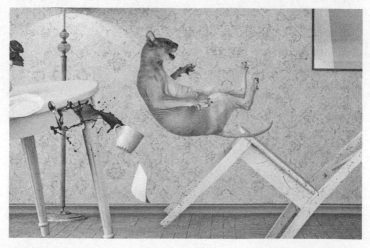

bear the weight of the impact, and their low body volume-to-weight ratio allows them to slow their speed when falling. Strangely, a 1987 study of 132 cats published in the *Journal of the American Veterinary Medical Association* found that cats were actually less likely to suffer severe injuries when they fell from a height of more than seven stories than when they fell from between two and seven stories. It was thought that after falling five stories, the cat reaches terminal velocity and then relaxes and spreads its body to increase drag. However, critics of the study pointed out a sampling error in that fatal falls were not included, as an already-dead cat would not be taken to the vet. Most experts now agree with the conclusion of a 2003 study of 119 cats that was published in the *Journal of Feline Medicine and Surgery*. It concluded that falls from more than seven stories were more likely to result in severe injury or death. Even though the cat is able to right itself and land on its feet, its legs are not able to absorb all the shock from such a fall.

So, while a cat will always land on its feet, it won't always survive; luckily, they've got nine lives. Of course, if you really want to test a cat's righting reflex, strap a piece of buttered toast to it back.

## WHY DON'T VULTURES GET SICK FROM EATING ROTTEN MEAT?

While many animals eat carrion, vultures are unique in that they eat carrion that is rotten. They will often wait for bacteria to decompose a dead body so that it's easier to eat, and they'll happily chow down on meat that contains anthrax, cholera, and even rabies. No other stomach in the animal kingdom can match the vulture's. How do they manage such a feat?

The main reason is that vultures have extremely acidic gastric juices that are strong enough to destroy the majority of bacteria that the birds ingest from rotten meat. The vulture's stomach acid is estimated to be up to 1,000 times stronger than a human's. It is even stronger than battery acid and is able to dissolve some metals. Vultures also urinate on the ground and on themselves as they eat. Owing to the highly acidic nature of their bodily waste,  any bacteria that gets on the bird's body is killed, and there's the added environmental benefit of sterilizing the area around the carcass, which prevents any disease from spreading.

The vulture also has one of the strongest immune systems of all animals, which acts to fight the deleterious effects of the bacteria it encounters and develops a tolerance toward deadly bacteria.

But why are vultures built this way? Evolution. The bird is descended from its carrion-eating ancestors. By necessity, vultures have been eating rotting bacteria-ridden flesh for thousands of years. Those that survived the deadly cocktail dominated the gene pool and produced offspring better equipped to do the same. The birds were progressively able to eat more and more decayed flesh without consequence, evolving into the modern-day vulture.

And while vultures have a poor reputation in many circles, being seen as synonymous with death and disease, they actually produce the opposite effect. When vulture populations decline in an area, the rate of disease usually increases. Vultures are known as dead-end hosts, meaning that if a vulture eats a diseased animal, the spread of disease ends there, as the bird neutralizes it. Vultures also pick carcasses completely clean, further reducing the risk of any disease spreading. When the number of vultures declined in parts of India in the 1980s, it led to an explosion of feral dogs and rats, with whom the vulture competes for carcasses. Unlike the dead-end vultures, these animals actually carry and spread disease.

So, the next time you frown upon the vulture in disgust, remember that they're an evolutionarily advanced bird and are actually doing us all a favor.

## WHY DON'T TORNADOES EVER HIT BIG CITIES?

When most people picture a tornado in their minds, they see the menacing signature spiral snaking its way across the plains, destroying everything in its path. But why are they always going across open countryside? Why don't they hit big cities?

They do. It's a common myth that tornadoes don't strike city areas. One basis for the myth is the argument that the tall skyscrapers in cities could affect the air flow patterns needed to sustain a tornado, but there is little basis for this. Tornadoes can reach 9 miles in height and over a mile across.

Such supercells would not be repelled by the buildings of a city.

The fact is that cities don't get hit as often as other areas because of their small size. Cities make up a very small percentage of the land compared to the open, less-populated areas of the country.

Climate plays the biggest role in whether a tornado forms or not. The Midwest, known as Tornado Alley, receives an abundance of warm, moist air from the Gulf of Mexico, warm and dry air from the west, and cool air from the north. The combination of these three types of air is perfect for tornado formation and is far different from the conditions on the east or west coasts, where population densities are higher in large cities like New York and Los Angeles. Within Tornado Alley, the population density is low and the cities are smaller, so the chances of a tornado hitting a city are low.

While the odds of a city being hit are low, tornadoes can travel anywhere, and cities do get hit. Both Dallas and Miami were hit in 1997, while Los Angeles has had thirty tornadoes since 1918. There are numerous other examples, including St. Louis. This large city in Missouri, right in the midst of Tornado Alley, has a long history of destructive tornadoes and has been hit twenty-two times in the past forty years.

## ❓ WHY DOESN'T YOUR OWN SNORING WAKE YOU UP?

It's a common gripe of women the world over: They lie there awake, suffering through a snore that could rival a chainsaw, while the offending male remains asleep, blissfully unaware of the disturbance he is causing. Is there anything more infuriating? Why doesn't the noise wake him up? (It's usually men who snore the most and the loudest.)

Most snoring occurs when a person is deeply asleep and hardest to arouse. Couple this with the way the brain processes sensory information during sleep. Our nervous system is continuously bombarded with information that it uses to control the many processes that keep us alive. When we are asleep, the brain continues to process vital information, such as telling the heart to beat and the lungs to breathe, but in order to get some rest, it ignores the sensory observations that are routine and not life-threatening. A part of the brain called the thalamus actively filters out these mundane noises

to enable us to sleep. Snoring, like the repetitive motion of a fan or the ticking of a clock, is one of those noises. However, if the brain senses danger, from something irregular like a fire alarm or someone calling your name, you are far more likely to wake up.

Mind you, it's not completely peaceful for the snorer. Research suggests that snorers are actually awakened quite regularly by their snoring but do not come to full consciousness and so don't remember waking up. For this reason, snoring may actually have a negative impact on sleep for both the person listening to it and the snorer himself.

##  WHY ARE RAIN CLOUDS DARK?

On a fine and sunny day, look to the sky and any clouds that you see will be white. But as soon as a storm starts building and rain is in the air, the clouds take on an ominous dark appearance. What causes this noticeable change?

The air around us is full of water in its gaseous form, called water vapor. When the air near the ground warms and starts to rise, it takes water vapor with it. As it rises higher into the sky, the air starts to cool, which causes the water vapor to condense as droplets onto atmospheric dust. These tiny particles join together to form clouds.

Cloud particles scatter all colors of light from the sun, which together make up white light. Thin clouds that do not contain a lot of moisture allow enough white sunlight through them so that they appear white to observers.

Rain clouds, however, are much thicker and denser because of all the water they contain. As sunlight enters the top of a cloud, it is scattered across the top of the cloud by the water droplets, resulting in less light penetrating all the way through. The particles on the underside of the cloud receive less light to scatter to our eyes. This makes the cloud appear gray or black from underneath. And the thicker the cloud, the darker it will appear.

## WHEN PEOPLE LOSE THEIR JOBS, WHY IS IT SAID THAT THEY GOT THE SACK OR GOT FIRED?

When someone loses their job, it is commonly said that they got the sack or got fired. How did these expressions originate?

Both relate to the tools that workers used to ply their trades. When tradesmen traveled from place to place looking for work, they generally owned their tools and carried them around in a large sack. Work was often irregular, so the tradesmen never knew how long they might be employed. At the start of any given job they would hand over their  sack to their employer to look after. The employer would keep the sack for the duration of the tradesman's employment. If the tradesman's services were no longer required and he was dismissed from the job, the employer would give him the sack.

To get fired originated from a time in England when miners carried their own tools from job to job. Like today, stealing was a serious offense, and any miner caught taking valuable materials, such as coal, tin, or another ore, was immediately dismissed. To prevent them from repeating their crime in another employment, their tools would also be confiscated and burned at the plant in full view of all the workers—their tools would literally get fired. Some suggest that the actual offender was set on fire in these instances, but it was likely just his tools.

To get fired was far harsher and more humiliating than to get the sack. The former was always the result of malicious behavior, while the latter was often the result of a lack of demand.

## WHY DO WE RARELY SEE DEAD BIRDS?

The United States is home to billions of birds spanning thousands of species. Although some birds, such as parrots, have long lives, most of the birds that we see, like finches and sparrows, live only a few years. Given that most birds have fairly short life spans, what happens when they die? Why don't we see thousands of bird carcasses lying around?

1. **Predators.** A lot of birds don't die from old age but are killed and eaten by predators, such as other birds or cats. These predators then consume the birds. In addition, any birds that do get weak or old become easy prey, and are killed and eaten before they die naturally.

2. **Migration.** A lot of birds migrate, and many die on the long flight, landing in lakes or oceans, where we don't notice them.

3. **Concealment.** Like many other animals, if birds feel sick or vulnerable, they will often seek out secluded places to hide away, such as a hole in a tree. There they will either recover or die, and if it's the latter, we won't see the remains.
4. **Decay.** Birds are light in weight, are thin skinned, have very little fat, and their bones are not dense. When a dead bird hits the ground, if it is not eaten or taken by a predator, it will be invaded by insects and bacteria that quickly decompose the carcass. Within only a few days, very little will be left that we can recognize as the remains of a bird.

## WHO DETERMINES THE BOUNDARY LINE BETWEEN OCEANS?

The world's oceanic waters constitute one global, interconnected body that covers 71 percent of the earth's surface. Sometimes referred to as the World Ocean, it is split into seven well-known oceans: the Indian, South Pacific, North Pacific, Southern, Arctic, North Atlantic, and South Atlantic. Given that these oceans are all joined together with no discernible boundaries, how are the divisions determined?

The International Hydrographic Organization (IHO) is an intergovernmental body representing hydrography. It ensures that the seas and oceans of the world are properly surveyed and charted. Before its incorporation, many countries had similar bodies that undertook this task, but the IHO became the unified and globally respected body.

Established in 1921 and recognized by the United Nations, the IHO plays a key role to establish the major oceanic divisions of the world. So, how do they do it?

The IHO principally uses continents, archipelagos, and the limits of other bodies of water as markers to determine where the oceans begin and end. To exemplify the application of these criteria, let's look at the Atlantic Ocean. Broadly speaking, it separates the Americas from Eurasia and Africa, and is further divided into northern and southern portions by the equator.

More specifically, this is a summary of how the 3rd and current edition of the IHO's *Limits of Oceans and Seas* defines the North Atlantic Ocean:

- **On the west:** Reaches the eastern limits of the Caribbean Sea, the southeastern limits of the Gulf of Mexico from the north coast of Cuba to Key West, the southwestern limit of the Bay of Fundy, and the southeastern and northeastern limits of the Gulf of St. Lawrence.
- **On the north:** Reaches the southern limit of Davis Strait from the coast of Labrador to Greenland, and the southwestern limit of the Greenland Sea and Norwegian Sea from Greenland to the Shetland Islands.
- **On the east:** Reaches the northwestern limit of the North Sea, the northern and western limits of the Scottish Seas, the southern limit of the Irish Sea, the western limits of the Bristol and English Channels of the Bay of Biscay, and the Mediterranean Sea.
- **On the south:** Reaches the equator, from the coast of Brazil to the southwestern limit of the Gulf of Guinea.

## ❓ DO CELL PHONES REALLY INTERFERE WITH AIRCRAFT?

"Please set all portable electronic devices, including any cell phones, to flight mode." How many times have you heard this? At the start and end of every flight. Most people comply with the instruction without being completely sure why. The general assumption is that the signals from cell phones interfere with the plane's navigational instruments, which might cause the plane to crash. Yet many people forget to turn their phones off, and the plane doesn't crash. This raises the question—can a cell phone really bring down a plane?

The Federal Communications Commission has banned the use of cell phones on aircraft, but that ban is to prevent the disruption to cellular towers on the ground. When a call is made from the air, the signal bounces off multiple available cell towers, rather than one at a time. This may result in the ground networks becoming clogged up. So, no danger to the plane there.

However, the Federal Aviation Association has banned the use of cell phones because of potential electromagnetic interference with the aircraft systems, caused by the signals cell phones emit. These may interrupt the normal operation of the plane's instruments, in particular the communication and navigation systems, and potentially the flight controls (such as autopilot) and warning systems.

But has this ever happened?

According to the International Air Transport Association, seventy-five instances of suspected electronic device interference occurred between 2003 and 2009. While these instances could not be definitively validated, the pilots who reported the incidents claimed that once the passengers were then instructed to turn off their electronic devices, the issues were resolved. That said, there is no known example of an air accident having been caused by the use of a cell phone. But it's also impossible to say that some accidents may not have been caused this way.

In a 2013 article in *CNN Travel* titled "Can Your Cell Phone Bring Down a Plane?" Kenny Kirchoff, an engineer at Boeing's Electromagnetic Interference Lab in Seattle, said that the issue is not necessarily that a phone can bring down a plane, but that a phone can interfere with the plane and cause more work for the pilots during the critical phases of flight. This may cause a pilot to get distracted, lowering the overall level of safety on the plane.

On balance, it's likely that cell phones can interfere with an aircraft, but only to a small degree. And if the risks were significant and life-threatening, the policy would be far more strictly enforced, or phones would be banned from aircraft entirely. That said, the consequences could be dire, so for the skeptics out there, perhaps this is one of those cases where it's better to be safe than sorry.

## WHAT ARE THE ORIGINS OF THE ENGLISH ALPHABET?

The English language is often considered one of the more difficult languages to master due to its many inconsistencies. Many of these have arisen through the complex development of the English alphabet, which involved several languages, multiple countries, and thousands of years.

The first true alphabet was created in Canaan, a Semitic-speaking region in the Ancient Near East, around 2000 BC.

 Replacing the complex system of Egyptian hieroglyphics (which isn't considered an alphabet), it contained between twenty-two and thirty-two letters, but no vowels. About 700 years later, the Phoenicians took this alphabet to Greece, where vowels were added around 750 BC. The Greek alphabet was the first true phonetic alphabet, meaning it had a letter to represent every sound in the language. The Greeks took this alphabet to Italy, where it evolved into the Latin alphabet that was used by the Roman Empire. By the 3rd century BC, it was very similar to modern English, containing every letter except J and W, with U and V being joined as one letter.

The English alphabet evolved in the 7th century AD, when the Latin alphabet was introduced to Britain by the Romans. At the time, Britain was controlled by the Anglo-Saxons, a Germanic tribe that spoke Old English and used a runic alphabet called *futhark*. The English alphabet formed as a combination of the Latin and Old English runic alphabets. After two hundred years of Norman influence since their invasion of 1066 AD, Britain's combined language became Middle English, with an alphabet of 26 letters, most of which were similar to those in modern English.

With the introduction of the printing press to Britain in the mid-15th century, the language became more standardized, and Modern English appeared. By the mid-16th century, the formerly joined U and V were split, with U becoming a vowel and V a consonant, and by about 1600, the letter J was introduced. This created the modern English 26-letter alphabet that we know today.

So, the next time you're reciting your ABCs as second nature, spare a moment to think about the long and circuitous path those letters have taken.

## WHY DOES OLD FILM FOOTAGE APPEAR TO BE IN FAST FORWARD?

Why is it that every time you see film footage of old silent movies, the actors are moving at breakneck speed and poor Charlie Chaplin looks like his pants are on fire as he darts across the screen?

Before movies had synchronized soundtracks, there was no standard frame rate. The rate depended on the operator, who hand-cranked the equipment. As a general rule, the average speed of silent movies was about sixteen frames per second (fps), although this varied quite a bit.

When sound was introduced in the 1920s, it was discovered that sixteen frames per second was too slow for accurate sound recording and playback, and a speed of twenty-four fps was needed to produce decent sound quality. The faster pace meant more sound information was recorded

per second, increasing the quality. For this reason, the standardized camera speed became twenty-four fps. When sixteen fps footage is projected using the modern twenty-four fps playback equipment, one second of film will play in two-thirds of a second. This makes it appear significantly faster.

So, it turns out that Charlie Chaplin was actually walking at a normal pace—it's just the modern equipment that makes him move like his pants are on fire.

## HOW DID THE EXPRESSION TEETOTAL ORIGINATE?

A teetotal is a person who completely abstains from alcohol. It seems a strange term to apply to such a person, so how did it come about?

Some believe that teetotal refers to a person who has given up alcohol and drinks tea as an alternative. But this is not the case. The spelling is different, for one.

The word actually derives from an Englishman named Richard Turner. In 1833, Turner gave a speech at a meeting of the Preston Temperance Society. He preached total abstention from alcohol, as opposed to just hard liquor, and in his speech said "tee-tee-tee-total." It is not known whether he had a speech impediment and was stammering, or whether his reduplication of the T was for emphasis, but the congregation embraced it, and teetotal soon became a commonplace word.

## WHY ARE BATTERIES NEVER INCLUDED?

Is there anything more frustrating when you're a kid than opening a new toy on Christmas morning, all excited, and immediately upon turning it on, nothing happens? It won't work no matter what you do. Then you see those tiny words on the side of the box, the death knell for all children: "Batteries Not Included." No! There'll be no stores open today. The day is ruined. Why not just include the batteries and save everyone some trouble?

Economics.

Electronic items are often made in foreign countries and have to be shipped and stored. The companies never know how long an item may sit in a warehouse or on the shelf of a store, so batteries may go dead or, worse, corrode and leak, ruining the item. If batteries were included, each electrical item would have to be given a shelf life, and companies don't want to do that unless necessary, as it would result in wasted stock.

There is also an issue with some shipping laws that regulate the transport of hazardous materials. Certain items with batteries in them may cost more to distribute, and companies are always looking for ways to avoid additional costs.

Finally, electronic and toy manufacturers save money if they don't pay extra for the batteries. If batteries were included, the company would have to form a partnership with a battery company or create a battery division of their own, resulting in a number of associated costs. So, they simply don't include the batteries.

No batteries makes complete financial sense for the manufacturing and distribution companies, but no sense at all to a disappointed kid on Christmas morning.

## ❓ WHY DO SEAGULLS HANG OUT IN PARKING LOTS?

Have you ever driven into a supermarket parking lot, hundreds of miles from the nearest ocean, and wondered why you're competing for a parking space with a flock of seagulls? Why are they there?

Seagulls are more accurately called gulls, and while they often like to be near water, they don't strictly live by the sea. There are more than fifty species of gulls, some of which live inland, including the ring-billed gull, which thrives in suburban settings.

But why congregate in parking lots? Two reasons:

1. **Food.** Gulls are opportunistic feeders and will eat almost anything available, including fish, insects,

fruits, and scraps discarded by humans. Parking lots tend to offer plenty of food scraps in and around their dumpsters and garbage cans, especially if there is a food outlet in the complex. The gulls in parking lots are also often the beneficiaries of a French fry or two thrown by a benevolent patron. Manicured grass and other landscaped patches around the pavements of parking lots are also a good source of insects and worms.

2. **Safety.** Parking lots are quite safe for gulls. They're spacious, open, and flat, and this gives the gulls a clear view in all directions, so they can see any approaching danger. The roof of a supermarket also provides a safe resting place, where they can fly to easily if a predator appears.

Gull populations have increased significantly as a result of the opportunities these parking lots afford them. Plus, for the teenage gulls, the parking lots are just a good place to meet and hang out. The only problem is that their parents are usually there doing the exact same thing.

## DO THE ESKIMOS REALLY HAVE HUNDREDS OF WORDS FOR SNOW?

The claim that the Eskimos have hundreds of words for snow is widespread but controversial. The idea came about as a result of anthropologist Franz Boas's travels through northern Canada in the 1880s to learn about the Eskimos. In his 1911 work, *Handbook of American Indian Languages*, Boas discussed the many words that the Eskimos used for snow, and the concept spread into popular culture. Some have labeled it the Great Eskimo Vocabulary Hoax, but is there actually any basis to the claim?

The two main Eskimo languages, Inuit and Yupik, both have multiple dialects. This fact alone gives rise to many different words for snow. But these languages are able to spawn so many words for snow primarily because they're polysynthetic. Polysynthetic languages combine a limited set of roots with multiple word endings to create many stand-alone words. Where in English, a concept such as "snow falling heavily and settling on the ground" is expressed as a sentence, the Eskimos will use a single word. For example, the root word *tla* means "snow that falls." Adding suffixes to this root gives any number of new single words: *tlamo* (snow that falls in large wet flakes); *tlatim* (snow that falls in small flakes); *tlaslo* (snow that falls slowly); *tlapinti* (snow that falls quickly); *tlapa* (snow that falls as powder snow); and *tlayinq* (snow that falls and is mixed with mud). That's just to name a few.

This means that Eskimos don't just have hundreds of words for snow, they have hundreds of words for everything, as an almost limitless number of single words can be formed using this grammatical structure.

So, how many words for snow are there?

Some linguists claim that the Yupik language has at least forty distinct words for snow, while the Inuit language has fifty-three. But it depends on what constitutes different words. If you're talking about the root words for snow, it's a similar number to what we have in English, where there is snow, sleet, powder, blizzard, slush, and so on. In an analysis of the Eskimo languages in 1991 by Professor Anthony Woodbury of the University of Texas in Austin, there were fifteen distinct root words for snow that would be considered separate words in English.

But if you're talking about the polysynthetic words, the number is limited only by an Eskimo's imagination. And with little else to look at in those parts aside from snow, that could run pretty wild. Let's just hope they've come up with a combined word for "yellow snow not to be eaten under any circumstances."

## WHAT IS THE BUTTERFLY EFFECT, AND HOW DID IT ORIGINATE?

The butterfly effect is the concept that very small causes can have very large effects; stated simply, the flap of a butterfly's wings in Brazil can set off a tornado in Texas. As far-fetched

as that seems, let's see if there's any truth to it.

Chaos theory, or the science of surprises, forms the basis of the butterfly effect. It deals with the unpredictable and the nonlinear, things that are impossible to control, like weather, turbulence, and the stock market. Initially, the effect was used with weather prediction, but later crossed into various scientific areas, as well as being used as a metaphor.

The main premise of the idea is that while a butterfly's wings don't directly power a tornado, they can cause one by initiating a process that cascades into large-scale events; a small change in the initial conditions can lead to drastic changes in the results.

Chaos theory began as early as 1800 when German philosopher Johann Fichte said, "You could not remove a single grain of sand from its place without thereby...changing something throughout all parts of the immeasurable whole." But it wasn't until 1963 that American mathematician and meteorologist Edward Lorenz coined the term. When running a numerical computer model to simulate a weather event, he rounded the initial condition data to a figure of 0.506 from the more precise figure of 0.506127. What he thought was an inconsequential change produced a completely different weather scenario.

But is there any basis for the seemingly implausible influence of the butterfly?

Not according to David Orrell, who has a doctorate in predicting nonlinear systems from the University of Oxford. In his 2006 book, *The Future of Everything: The Science of Prediction,* he describes the extreme difficulty meteorologists face in predicting the weather. Because it is so sensitive to changes in atmospheric conditions, like temperature and pressure, the weather cannot be accurately forecast more than a few days in advance. An estimation of the temperature that is wrong by just a fraction of a degree can lead to a cascade of errors that results in a completely different weather event. However, Orrell added that "the changes that make a difference are far bigger than a butterfly flapping its wings." Each flap of the wings causes a tiny change in the air pressure around the butterfly, but this fluctuation is insignificant compared with the air's total pressure, which is around 100,000 times larger. The surrounding air molecules easily absorb the flap of the wings so that only a few inches away from the butterfly, the turbulence it creates will be damped out and irrelevant.

So, while very small weather events, such as a slight change in temperature or the movement of an individual cloud, can produce drastic changes, the notion of a butterfly flapping its wings eventually resulting in a tornado is a poetic one, and completely fanciful.

What all this means is that now we know that the butterfly isn't at fault, we can keep blaming the weatherman when the weekend is spoiled by unforeseen rain.

## WHY DOESN'T GLUE GET STUCK IN THE BOTTLE?

It's a mystery that has confounded many a student for decades. Glue sticks things together, but it doesn't stick to the inside of the bottle. Why not?

It's not magic; it's science.

The white glue used by most students is made up of a variety of chemicals called polymers. These polymer molecules bind together to make glue stick. However, the glue also contains a solvent, such as water or acetone. The solvent keeps the glue in a liquid form.

Once the glue is squeezed from the bottle, the solvent is exposed to the air and evaporates. As it evaporates, the glue dries and hardens as the chemical bonds in the polymers are joined in a process called mechanical adhesion.

White glue doesn't stick to the inside of the bottle because there is not enough air in there to make the solvent evaporate. The bottle protects the glue from the air and keeps it liquid. That's why, if you leave the lid off the bottle, the glue will harden. This can also happen when the bottle gets close to empty. In that case, there is more air inside the bottle, which evaporates the water and makes the glue set.

Super glue tends to dry out in its container far more readily than white glue. That's because, instead of polymers, super glue is made of a chemical called cyanoacrylate. Cyanoacrylate binds things together when it reacts with water vapor in the air, in a process called chemical adhesion. As all air contains water vapor, the glue container must be tightly sealed to prevent any vapor from seeping in and reacting with the glue.

In the end, keeping glue wet in the bottle is all about water. With white glue, you need to keep the water in the glue, and with superglue, you need to keep the water out.

## WHY DO BATS ROOST UPSIDE DOWN?

Remember as a kid when you'd hang upside down from the monkey bars in the playground? Within a few minutes, the blood would rush to your head, your hands would hurt, and you'd have to get down. Imagine spending the whole day that way. Welcome to the world of the bat. Why do they do it?

1. **Bone structure.** Bats have lightweight bones in their hind legs that are unable to support the bat's bodyweight in an upright stance. As they cannot stand on a branch like a bird, they hang upside down instead.

2. **Take off.** The wings of bats don't produce enough lift to take off from a dead stop, and their hind legs don't have the strength to build up enough speed for a running take off. This leaves the bat no choice but to hang from an elevated position and fall into flight. This provides the added advantage of allowing the bat to escape quickly if threatened. By hanging upside down, they are already in the perfect position to simply spread their wings and fly away.

3. **Safety.** Hanging upside down in secluded places is an effective way to hide from predators. This is particularly important because bats sleep during the day, when many predators, such as eagles, are hunting.

   Bats usually roost in places that few other animals can reach, such as a cave, where there is no option other than to hang upside down, so it provides them ample protection. There is also little competition for these roosting spots, as they are not typically areas where it would be possible for birds to build a nest.

Don't feel too sorry for the bats though. They have a unique physiological adaptation that allows them to hang upside down without exerting any energy. The tendons in a bat's talons are connected to its upper body, and not a muscle. When a bat gets into position, the bat relaxes and the weight of the bat pulls down on the tendons, causing the talons to clench. A bat only has to exert energy when it wants to fly away, flexing its muscles to release its grip. Plus, it gets to sleep all day while the rest of us are at work.

## ❓ WHY ARE SOME PEOPLE DOUBLE-JOINTED?

In every classroom there is always the guy who can bend his fingers back freakishly far, and then brag about being double-jointed. But is there actually such a thing?

The term double-jointed implies that a person has twice the number of joints, giving them unusual flexibility, but that's not the case. People have the same number of joints, but those who can contort their fingers or limbs like a pretzel generally have what's called hypermobility syndrome. People are born with this ability, and it doesn't come through practice.

Two factors affect the motion of a joint: ligaments and bones. Most joints are wrapped in ligaments that connect bone to bone, and tendons, that connect muscle to bone. If a person has naturally loose ligaments and tendons, they will be able to move their limbs farther than average.

The bones in many joints have a ball and socket; the domed bone rolls inside a curved socket. It is this joint that gives your arm such a wide range of motion. People with hypermobility syndrome often have very shallow sockets (or a small domed bone), which allow the domed bone the ability to move more freely, giving the limb greater mobility. Sometimes the ball part of the joint can actually be moved completely out of its socket, which allows the person to painlessly dislocate their shoulder. Now, there's a party trick!

Hypermobility tends to diminish with age, and there is evidence that people of African, Asian, and Middle Eastern descent are more likely to be hypermobile than those of European descent.

While the condition rarely causes any pain, a flexible joint is not as stable as a normal one, and so generally requires a person to use more energy in stabilizing themselves, inhibiting them from doing the actions they intend. For this reason, hypermobility can be more of a liability than an asset for athletes or professional dancers.

## WHY DON'T LIZARDS GET SUNBURNED?

Why is it that a lizard can bask on a rock in the blazing sun all day and remain unaffected, but if we go out there for an hour we look like a cooked lobster? What stops them from getting sunburned?

Two reasons: scales and gadusol. You've heard of the first, but probably not the second.

The epidermis of the lizard is protected from the harmful ultraviolet rays of the sun by its scales. These act as a protective barrier, but also function to retain moisture underneath.

But in addition to their scales, lizards have evolved another means of protecting themselves from UV rays. They produce a natural compound called gadusol that shields them from the burning sun just as sunscreen would. A 2015 study led by Professor Taifo Mahmud from Oregon State University found that many reptiles, as well as fish and birds, can naturally produce gadusol, originally thought to be obtained from consuming certain algae and bacteria. In addition to providing ultraviolet protection, gadusol was also found to act as an antioxidant and help with stress relief.

The genetic machinery to make gadusol is lacking in humans and other mammals, but because it is a naturally produced compound, Professor Mahmud believes it may be developed into pill form to provide these benefits to people.

And it's obviously an impressive compound, as any lizard would typically die from overheating before any threat of sunburn became an issue. But they don't care anyway—the gadusol makes them very relaxed as well.

# ❓ WHY DON'T WOMEN FAINT AS MUCH AS THEY USED TO?

If you watch any period drama from the 1800s, the women seem to drop like flies, struggling to maintain consciousness when confronted with the slightest emotional shock. These days, women rarely faint at all. Have women evolved to lose the fainting gene, or is something else really going on?

Here are a number of explanations for this era's fainting disparity:

1. **Corsets.** Women in Victorian times often wore corsets, made of tightly woven fabric with vertical rib inserts and fastened at the back with tight laces. These garments were worn to give a flat look to the stomach and to accentuate certain bodily curves. But they also made it hard for the wearer to breathe or eat (because it was hard to get food down, or the stomach was so compressed that it couldn't hold much food), and the woman's heart was unable to pump as freely. During times of heightened emotional arousal, the body needs more oxygen to fuel the fight-or-flight reflex, and the corset prevented this. A lady wearing a corset in such circumstances wouldn't have been able to breathe as well, and with potentially low blood sugar from a lack of food, she would have been more likely to get lightheaded and faint.

2. **Heat and weight.** Women of that era also wore an enormous amount of clothing, even in summer. In addition to the corset, they wore underwear, a full skirt, a petticoat, and a bonnet. Bearing the excess

weight, women may have overheated more than today, causing them to faint more readily.

3. **Poisoning.** During the 19th century, arsenic was widely used in the manufacture of everything from fabrics to paints to wallpaper to makeup. Lead was also a common ingredient in makeup and hair dyes. These prevalent toxins could have resulted in the chronic poisoning of women, who swooned and fainted as a consequence.

4. **Femininity.** While all of the above factors may well have contributed to a higher incidence of fainting in yesteryear, it is highly likely that many fainting fits were simply put on. Women, particularly those of high standing, were expected to play the role of the delicate flower, and it was considered ladylike to faint if their slightest sensibility was offended. These days, fainting by women is generally seen as a sign of weakness and is not something a man finds attractive. That fact alone may have been enough to quash the pastime.

## WHY DOES THE PRICE OF GAS END IN NINE-TENTHS OF A CENT?

At all gas stations in the United States, if you have a powerful set of binoculars and look through them carefully enough, you'll see a miniature nine underlined and raised next to the main part of the gas price. That nine is shorthand for nine-tenths of a cent, or $0.009. Why on earth do they do that?

Two reasons: tax and marketing.

In 1932, the United States Congress implemented a gas tax as a temporary measure to reduce the deficits acquired during the Great Depression. Various states then starting introducing a gas tax. The fuel companies were not willing to bear the full burden of these taxes, so they decided to pass the costs on to the consumer in the form of a price hike. They did this by adding nine-tenths of a cent to the price of gas, which was significantly more than the tax they had to pay. But why not round it up to a full cent?

Marketing. Pricing gas to nine-tenths of a cent is similar to when stores sell items for prices ending in 99 cents. Consumers tend to place a much greater emphasis on the first number in a price and ignore the latter, less significant numbers. Something priced at $7.99 seems a lot cheaper than $8, because the seven is the number that is focused on. Similarly, when filling up with gas, customers typically only pay attention to the first three digits of a price, so that $2.49 and nine-tenths gives the impression that the cost is only $2.49, when it is essentially $2.50. This sort of strategy was particularly important during the Great Depression, when most people were under serious financial pressure.

And like most practices that result in more money for large companies, once the Great Depression was over, the extra nine-tenths remained, and probably always will. But just how much does that fraction add up to anyway? Around $400 million every year.

## ❓ WHY ARE RABBITS ASSOCIATED WITH EASTER?

Every Easter, millions of children (and a lot of chocolate-loving adults) bite the heads off their Easter Bunnies with glee. But why did this animal become associated with Easter in the first place?

The exact reason the rabbit was selected is uncertain. In general the animal is known to be a prolific procreator and was an ancient symbol of fertility and new life.

People of ancient times believed that the hare and rabbit were hermaphrodites and could reproduce without copulating, probably because these animals can conceive a second litter of offspring while still pregnant with the first.

This led to an association with the Virgin Mary and the hare becoming a popular motif in medieval church art.

Some suggest that the Easter Bunny derives from Ostara, the ancient Germanic fertility goddess. Ostara was the friend of all children, and to amuse them, she changed her pet bird into a rabbit, which brought forth brightly colored eggs that Ostara gave to the children as gifts. The association between the Easter Bunny and Ostara began with the English monk Venerable Bede, whose 8th-century work, *The Reckoning of Time,* stated that the word Easter stemmed from Eostre, another version of the name Ostara. There is, however, little other evidence to support this origin.

Originally called the Easter Hare, the concept likely originated with the German Lutherans, with whom the animal played the role of judge, determining whether children had been good or bad at the start of the season of Eastertide. The legend has it that the Hare would then carry colored eggs in a basket and deliver them to children who had been good, similar to Santa Claus at Christmas. The earliest reference to an egg-toting Easter Bunny was in a 1572 German text that read "Do not worry if the Easter Bunny escapes you; should we miss his eggs, we will cook the nest." The custom was then mentioned in a 1682 text by the German physician Georg Franck von Franckenau.

In the 18th century, German immigrants took the custom of the Easter Bunny to the United States, and by the end of the 19th century, American stores in the eastern states were selling rabbit-shaped candy. This practice soon spread worldwide before the rabbits turned into chocolate.

# WHAT ARE THE ORIGINS OF THE PI SYMBOL?

Pi, written as π, the Greek letter for P, is the bane of many a child's primary school years. Simply put, it is the ratio of the circumference of any circle to the diameter of that circle. Regardless of the circle's size, if you divide the circumference by the diameter, it will always equal pi, which is approximately 3.14. But pi is an irrational number, which means that its decimal form never ends, nor becomes recurring. Incredibly, pi also connects the radius of a circle (which is half the diameter) to the area of that circle; the area is equal to pi times the radius squared. So, just how did this arcane mathematical beast come about?

Just like the known digits of pi when written out, its history is long. Mathematicians have been grappling with the concept for 4,000 years. By 2000 BC, the Babylonians and the Egyptians were aware of its existence, recognizing that every circle had the same ratio of circumference to diameter. A Babylonian tablet from 1900 to 1680 BC shows a value of 3.125 for pi, while the *Rhind Papyrus*, an Egyptian document from 1650 BC, gave a value of 3.1605. By the time of Ancient Greece in the 3rd century BC, Archimedes of Syracuse had approximated the value of pi to 3.1418, by far the closest up to that point.

About 400 years later, another Greek, Ptolemy, used the chords of a circle to produce 3.14166. A similar approach was used by the Chinese mathematician Zu Chongzhi in the 5th century AD, who calculated pi to nine decimal places. In about 1600, the German-Dutch mathematician Ludolph

Van Ceulen made it to 35 decimal places, and by 1701, the Englishman John Machin produced 100 digits.

In 1706, the Anglo-Welsh philologist William Jones began using the π symbol, and in 1768, Johann Heinrich Lambert, the Swiss polymath, proved that pi is an irrational number. In 1873, the amateur British mathematician William Shanks had reached 500 digits, and in 1882, the German Carl Louis Ferdinand von Lindemann proved that pi is transcendental, meaning that it can't be expressed in any finite series and "using a fixed-size font, it can't be written on a piece of paper as big as the universe."

Even today, despite 4,000 years and the thoughts, theories, proofs, and calculations from some of the world's best minds from multiple countries, pi's precise value still eludes us. But because of computers, at least we've got the first six billion decimal places.

And to celebrate that fact, March 14 is International Pi Day. Beware the pis of March.

# WHO WAS DR. PEPPER?

Everybody knows the carbonated soft drink called Dr Pepper. But who was the good doctor?

The drink was created in 1885 by a pharmacist named Charles Alderton. He worked at a drugstore in Waco, Texas, owned by Wade Morrison. After repeated sample testing by the two men, they began offering it to customers at the store, who would ask for a "Waco." But Morrison thought it needed a catchier name.

Morrison is credited with naming the drink Dr Pepper, but the origin for this name is uncertain, with even the company itself and the Dr Pepper museum being unsure. Theories include the following:

1. **Pepsin.** One theory is that the "pep" refers to pepsin, an enzyme sometimes used as a food additive. An old ledger book filled with formulae and recipes was discovered in an antique store in 2009. Several sheets in the book bore the name of Morrison's drugstore, and one recipe was titled "D Peppers Pepsin Bitters." It was speculated that this may have been an early recipe for the soft drink; however, Dr Pepper Snapple Group, the current manufacturer of the drink, insisted that it was never the formula, but a medicinal recipe for a digestive aid.

2. **Pep up.** Like many sodas at the time, Dr Pepper was marketed as an energizing pick-me-up tonic, leading some to suggest that it was named for the "pep" it gave to the people who drank it.

3. **Dr. Charles T. Pepper.** Morrison may have named the drink after this man, who gave him a job in Rural Retreat, Virginia. Others say that Dr. Pepper had also given Morrison permission to marry his daughter, but she was only eight years old when Morrison left for Texas, so this aspect of the story is likely false.

4. **Another Dr. Pepper.** Census records show young Morrison worked as a pharmacy clerk in Christiansburg, Virginia, and lived near a Dr. Pepper. The drink may have been named after that man.

While we will probably never know its true beginnings, the drink was very likely named after one of the Dr. Peppers that Morrison knew. Regardless, the drink was first marketed nationally in the United States in 1904 and became a huge success. The period after "Dr" was discarded for stylistic reasons in the 1950s.

## ? CAN PIRANHAS REALLY DEVOUR A COW IN UNDER A MINUTE?

Piranhas are among the most feared aquatic animals on earth. One of the reasons for this is President Theodore Roosevelt. When visiting Brazil in 1913, Teddy witnessed the piranha at work and reported what he saw in his 1914 book, *Through the Brazilian Wilderness*. He described the fish as the "embodiment of evil ferocity." What he had seen was a school of piranhas in the Amazon River tearing a cow apart and eating it to the bone in a matter of minutes. What he didn't realize was that the local fishermen had created the spectacle by blocking off part of the river and starving the fish for several days before pushing a dead cow into the water. But Roosevelt was a famous man, and his story was widely read. The legend of the piranha had begun, and in the ensuing years, Hollywood did the rest. So, can they do it?

The most vicious of the twenty species found in the Amazon is the red-bellied piranha. It is around 10 inches long and weighs about 3 pounds. But it's got some teeth. Its teeth are only about a quarter-inch long, but they're like razors, spaced in an interlocking pattern that cut like scissors. They also have incredibly strong jaws, capable of severing a human toe in one bite, and their muscular bodies allow for extremely rapid bursts of speed. In addition, piranhas don't chew. They bite off a chunk of flesh, which they immediately swallow, allowing them to bite off another chunk without delay.

These anatomical factors make the piranha an impressive predator, but their real strength is in numbers. They eat in schools of hundreds, continuously rotating during the feeding frenzy. They take turns at biting with incredible speed, often giving the water a boiling effect. But they only eat like this when they're starving, like in the scene that Roosevelt witnessed. So, while they are able to strip a beast quickly to its skeleton, they will only do so in very specific circumstances.

In reality, piranhas pose very little threat to humans or any large animals. They are extremely timid omnivores, usually scavenging on plants or dead or dying animals, and the main reason they travel in large schools is for protection via safety in numbers. They are certainly not in the habit of attacking living things that are many times their own size.

But if those very specific circumstances do exist, featuring a starving shoal of hundreds of piranhas, you'd best not get in the water. It has been estimated that a human could be stripped of flesh in five minutes by between 300 and 500 fish.

A cow would take a little longer, but they could do it. And whether it takes one minute or ten minutes really seems beside the point.

## WHY ARE PEOPLE IMMUNE TO THEIR OWN BODY ODOR?

Many scientists believe that the smells we emit played a key role in the propagation of our ancestors. The hair under our arms and in our genital area was used to trap pheromones, the chemical scents produced by the apocrine sweat glands in those regions. Those scents were the product of bacteria feeding on the proteins and oils we exuded, and each person provided a unique smell to attract a mate. All this may have worked many thousands of years ago, but today, we just call it body odor, and there's nothing sexy about it. But why can't we smell our own?

We are immune to our own body odor because of a phenomenon known as olfactory adaptation. The nose helps you to quickly detect things that are new and strange. There is an evolutionary basis for this. Any change to the surroundings of our ancestors could have represented a threat, and a change in smell may have signaled danger. Even today, our brains focus on new sights, sounds, feelings, and smells. But we adapt quickly. After a short period of exposure to the same smell, the nose is not as sensitive to it. The brain interprets any monotonous smell as not posing any danger, and so you simply stop smelling it. The smell becomes part of the base background scent and allows the nose to smell other, newer scents.

That's what happens with body odor. Because we are constantly smelling our own odor, the nose becomes accustomed to it. There's no way to get away from it, so the nose is unable to regain sensitivity to that smell.

The fact that it's difficult to smell your own body odor can make some people very defensive. They simply don't believe it when someone tells them they smell, so they don't do anything about it and go on smelling. But there are two things you should always remember when it comes to body odor: Whatever you can smell on yourself is far stronger to other people, and if someone tells you that you stink, take heed, because you probably do.

## WHY DO THE CHINESE USE CHOPSTICKS?

There is a lot of history behind chopsticks, the common eating utensil in China. Belief holds they were invented in ancient China around 9,000 years ago, prior to the Xia dynasty. The earliest evidence is a set of six chopsticks, each made of bronze and 10 inches long. They were found at the Ruins of Yin near Anyang and date to about 1200 BC. In the late Shang dynasty in 1100 BC, the tyrannical King Zhou ordered his craftsmen to make chopsticks from elephants' teeth as a mark of his wealth and power. The chopstick has obviously been taken very seriously in China for a long time. But why were they used in the first place?

The first chopsticks were likely made from twigs or bamboo and were probably not used as eating utensils, but rather for reaching into pots of hot water or oil, stirring the fire, and serving pieces of food. Steaming or boiling food was common in ancient China, and chopsticks were better suited than spoons when it came to lowering vegetables into the broth.

It wasn't until the Ming dynasty in around 1300 that chopsticks came into common use for both cooking and eating. They were given the name *kuaizi* and were considered safer for the mouth than sharp eating utensils. Apart from the chopstick's natural progression from a cooking to an eating implement, there was another key factor. The population boom across the country meant that both food and fuel for cooking became scarce. So that it would cook faster, people began cutting their food into tiny pieces. These bite-sized pieces rendered table knives obsolete. Knives also fell out of favor because of the teachings of Confucius, who was a vegetarian and against knives at the table.

In addition, chopsticks were, and still are, well-suited to Chinese food. Apart from the small pieces that are easy to pick up, the rice they eat is full of gummy starches that make it clump together. This makes chopsticks the perfect utensil to pick it up using one hand.

Over the years, a number of taboos have developed in relation to chopsticks. They should not be hit on the side of the bowl to make a lot of noise, as the Chinese believe only beggars do this in an attempt to procure a meal. You also shouldn't stretch out your index finger along the chopstick, as this can be interpreted as a kind of accusation to others. It is considered poor breeding to suck the ends of the chopsticks. And, whatever you do, don't insert the chopsticks vertically into your bowl. The Chinese only do this when they burn incense as a sacrifice to the dead.

## HOW WAS THE 1919 BASEBALL WORLD SERIES FIXED?

The Black Sox Scandal was a Major League Baseball match fixing incident in which eight members of the Chicago White Sox were accused of taking money from gamblers in exchange for intentionally losing the 1919 World Series against the Cincinnati Reds. With so much attention on the sport, how did one of the most notorious scandals in sporting history come about?

It all started with tension in the White Sox clubhouse. The players were divided into two factions that almost never spoke to each other, and the only common ground was their hatred of Charles Comiskey, the club's owner. Comiskey had a long reputation for underpaying his players, who were not able to change teams without permission. Gamblers were always on the lookout for players who wanted to make some extra cash, and one of the factions of the White Sox players was approached.

The players in on the scandal held a meeting in Chick Gandil's room at the Ansonia Hotel in New York. They agreed to go ahead. Soon after, rumors began circulating among gamblers that the series was fixed when a sudden

influx of money was bet on the Reds. Correspondents from the press box also heard the rumors and paid close attention to the players' performances.

On the second pitch of the series, Eddie Cicotte struck the hitter Morrie Rath in the back, delivering a prearranged signal confirming that the fix was going ahead. After Game 5, the White Sox were trailing the series 4 to 1, but the gamblers had reneged on their promised progress payments. In protest, the Sox won Games 6 and 7, but before Game 8, the gamblers made threats of violence. The White Sox lost Game 8 and the series on October 9, 1919.

*"Shoeless" Joe Jackson (top) and Kenesaw Mountain Landis, first Commissioner of Baseball (bottom)*

Rumors of the fix continued after the series, and in September 1920, a grand jury convened. Eddie Cicotte and "Shoeless" Joe Jackson both confessed their involvement. Eight players and five gamblers were indicted on nine counts of conspiracy to defraud. The trial began in June 1921. Cicotte and Jackson recanted their earlier confessions, and their signed statements went missing. The jury deliberated for less than three hours before returning verdicts of not guilty for all the players.

But it wasn't over yet. The fallout from the scandal resulted in the appointment of respected federal judge, Kenesaw Mountain Landis, as the first Commissioner of Baseball. Landis was granted absolute control over the sport, and despite the acquittals, he permanently banned all eight players from professional baseball. That ban remains in force to this day.

The eight banned players were Arnold "Chick" Gandil, Eddie Cicotte, Oscar "Happy" Felsch, Fred McMullin, George "Buck" Weaver, Charles "Swede" Risberg, Claude "Lefty" Williams, and "Shoeless" Joe Jackson. All of these players underperformed in the series, except for Jackson, who maintained his innocence until his death in 1951. Jackson had a series-leading .375 batting average, including the only home run, threw out five base runners, and handled thirty chances in the outfield with no errors. He did, however, bat far worse in the five games that the White Sox lost, hitting .286 in those games. Years later, the other banned players all said that Jackson was never present at any of the meetings with the gamblers.

With many of their best players sidelined, the White Sox dropped to seventh place in 1921 and did not win another American League Championship until 1959, nor another World Series until 2005. Many referred to their long lack of success as the Curse of the Black Sox.

# ❓ WHY ARE LARGE TRUCKS CALLED "SEMIS"?

 Have you ever wondered why the large trucks that traverse America's highways have so many names? Big rig and 18-wheeler are two self-explanatory nicknames, but why are they often called semis? There's nothing semi about these behemoths of the road.

The semi name is not related to the size of the truck, but to the trailer that it pulls. Here are two reasons for the name:

1. It's actually a semi-trailer, but people call them semis for short. A full trailer has both front and rear axles and is towed by a truck. This is how you tow a boat with a car. A semi-trailer, on the other hand, has no front wheels, and the front of the trailer rests on the rear of the truck.

2. The name also stems from the hitch that holds the truck and the trailer together. The name semi is an abbreviation for semi-oscillating turntable hitch. This semi-hitch connects to and sits on a greased turntable-like structure on top of the truck's rear axle. The semi-oscillating nature of the hitch allows the trailer to rotate horizontally and vertically, which is essential when turning corners. While a fully oscillating turntable hitch exists, allowing for every possible rotation, it is less common, and the semi-hitch is the norm.

## WHAT ARE THE ORIGINS OF THE EXPRESSION "DON'T LOOK A GIFT HORSE IN THE MOUTH"?

If someone tells you that you shouldn't look a gift horse in the mouth, they are telling you not to be critical or ungrateful for a gift. But given that very few people receive horses as a gift, where did this expression originate?

"Don't look a gift horse in the mouth" derives from racehorses and, in general, horses. Horses were always considered valuable, but there were very few ways of assessing a horse's age before purchase. It was a risk to buy a racehorse that was past its prime or a workhorse that was old.

The most reliable way of determining a horse's age is from its teeth. As a horse ages, its teeth wear down, but they also protrude forward, and its gums recede. If a horse was given to you, it was rude to look that gift horse in the mouth because this suggested you were assessing its value when you should have just been grateful for the gift.

This is also the derivation of the expression "straight from the horse's mouth" to describe first-hand information, as well as "long in the tooth," another equine tooth–related phrase meaning that someone is old.

# WHY IS JACK THE NICKNAME FOR JOHN?

Apart from the first letter and the fact that they are both monosyllabic, the names Jack and John have nothing in common, so how did Jack become a nickname for John?

Here are three theories:

1. John is a name that stretches back to biblical times. During the Middles Ages, the name John was altered slightly by Germanic tongues to Jan. When the Normans invaded England, they added "kin" to the end of the name to make a diminutive. Little John became Jankin, which turned into Jakin, and eventually Jack.

2. During medieval times, Jack was a generic name for a peasant. Over time, Jack worked its way into various words because of this: lumberjack, steeplejack, and even jackass, a term commonly used for a donkey. John, too, was used as a generic name for a person, as in John Doe, someone whose name was not known. The link between the two resulted in Jack being used for John.

3. Just as John was used as a generic name in England, Jacques was used for the same purpose in France. Because of this, the two names may have become related.

It is unknown which of these theories is correct, but it's likely that the two names will forever be joined. Besides, if they weren't, we'd be calling President Kennedy "John" instead of "Jack," and that just doesn't sound as cool.

## DO SKUNKS THINK SKUNKS STINK?

If you've ever seen the *Looney Tunes* cartoon character, Pepé Le Pew, you may well have the view that skunks relish their own stench, never allowing it to reduce their self-esteem. But is there any truth to this Warner Bros. depiction, or do skunks, too, find their odor offensive?

There are eleven species of skunks, but it's not the skunk itself that smells. Rather, it's what they spray as a defense from predators, such as foxes, badgers, and wolves. By using an oil gland adjacent to their anus, skunks shoot a plume of chemicals called thiols. These thiols are sulfur compounds that can cause headaches and burning in the eyes. Skunks can aim with surprising force and can accurately hit a target up to 10 feet away. But the worst part about their spray is the smell, which can linger on a victim

for weeks. Sometimes described as a combination of garlic, rotten eggs, and burnt rubber, the smell acts as a significant deterrent to predators, with even large bears keeping their distance.

But what about other skunks? According to Dr. Jerry Dragoo, the head of the Dragoo Institute for the Betterment of Skunks and Skunk Reputations, skunks do not find their odor pleasant at all. Skunks have a very strong sense of smell and find the odor offensive. If a skunk is hit by the spray, it will rub its face in the dirt or try to groom itself to remove the irritant. Out of courtesy, however, skunks rarely spray each other, except during mating season. In the 2016 *Mental Floss* article, "Do Skunks Know They Stink?," Dragoo said, "As for their own scent, when skunks spray, they rarely get any on themselves, but it does happen. Though they can tolerate their own smell, they do not appreciate getting it in the face and eyes."

For this reason and the fact that after five uses they have to wait about ten days to replenish their stocks, skunks use their spray reluctantly and will usually resort to hissing, foot-stamping, and threatening postures before unleashing the stench. But when they do, look out—no animal, including a skunk, wants to be hit.

So, as it turns out, the Warner Bros. cartoons may not be as scientifically accurate as many people once thought.

## WHY ARE BLUE JEANS SEWN WITH ORANGE THREAD?

In 1853, a twenty-four-year-old German-Jewish immigrant named Levi Strauss arrived in San Francisco to set up a Californian branch of his family's New York City dry goods business. To take advantage of the gold rush population, he brought a great deal of canvas for making wagon covers and tents. Strong pants were hard to find in the mining towns, and Strauss soon started making jeans from the canvas. The orange thread was intentionally selected, but it wasn't originally envisioned by the young entrepreneur.

Jacob Davis was a Latvian-born tailor from Reno, Nevada, who bought his material from Levi Strauss. In 1870, a woman asked Davis to make an incredibly strong pair of pants for her husband, a large man whose pants were prone to wearing out quickly. Davis decided to reinforce the pocket corners, where pants were  generally stressed, with copper rivets he had been using to attach straps to horse blankets. The customer liked the pants, so Davis made more, and within eighteen months had sold 200 pairs. Davis wanted to patent the idea, but didn't have the $68 fee. He sought a business partner and approached Levi Strauss. Strauss agreed, and the two men registered a patent in 1873. Davis began working for Strauss and ensured that the seams were sewn with orange thread to match the color of the copper rivets.

The rear pockets were also stitched with a unique and elaborate pattern. Originally lined with cotton, the orange stitching prevented the padding in the pockets from buckling. The cotton lining was later removed, but the orange stitching remained. It was only during World War II that the stitching was stopped, as it was considered wasteful during the lean times, but to maintain the tradition during that time, the orange design was hand painted.

To this day, the copper rivets, with matching orange thread and ornate, rear-pocket stitching, still grace every pair of Levi's produced. And many other companies have copied the winning formula.

# ❓ WHY WERE PREHISTORIC ANIMALS SO BIG?

While there were many small animals in prehistoric times, the land was dominated by oversized versions of our modern animals—giant snakes, giant sharks, giant birds, and really giant lizards. What was it about that era that made the animals so massive?

A number of environmental factors could account for their size.

1. In cold climates, a large frame can assist a warm-blooded animal in retaining heat, and in hot climates, a bigger mass can help insulate a cold-blooded animal and stop it from overheating.

2. Higher oxygen content in the air and more space in which to live may have contributed to their size.

3. Some scientists believe that the size of plant-eating dinosaurs may have been caused by the tough and woody foliage they were eating. The animals needed a large digestive tract to allow more time for bacteria to break down the food, and this led to a larger animal overall.

All of these theories may have some validity, but the most common reason cited by experts is simple: time. The animals had more time to grow, and given evolution, animals tend to get larger over millions of years. This is known as Cope's rule, named after the 19th-century paleontologist Edward Cope. Being larger than other animals of a species tends to offer an evolutionary advantage, allowing an animal to fight for territory, food, and mates, as well as making them less vulnerable to predation. Natural selection drives many animals to become larger over time.

While prehistoric animals generally became very large, they didn't all appear at the same time. The biggest dinosaurs lived during the Jurassic and Cretaceous Periods,  around 65 million to 200 million years ago. After they were wiped out, smaller animals took their place, growing larger over time to turn into impressive beasts like the woolly mammoth and saber-toothed tiger. They lived during the last ice age, which lasted between 2.6 million and 12,000 years ago. Each time a set of animals is devastated, it takes millions of years for the next generation to grow big again. The last major extinction took place around 12,000 years ago, which is not nearly enough time for animals to grow massive again. But, given enough time, they probably will.

Which makes you wonder just how big the blue whale will end up, as it is the largest animal ever to have existed.

## ❓ WHY DO SOME OLD PEOPLE CONSTANTLY MAKE A CHEWING MOTION?

It's hard not to stare any time you see an old person constantly chewing, but without any food in their mouth.

What causes some old people to engage in this weird and off-putting practice?

The constant chewing motion is almost always associated with elderly people who have lost their teeth. Most experts agree that the motion is a neuromuscular response by the oral cavity to try to reach an equilibrium. A full set of teeth helps to keep the jaws in place, but without teeth, it is difficult to position the jaws comfortably. Similarly, without any teeth, the tongue is not as confined and spreads out. In a subconscious effort to try to find a place for the tongue, the appearance of chewing is produced.

People with dentures can experience a similar problem. After living for years with normal teeth, wearing dentures can feel abnormal and lead to a restless chewing motion, often practiced unknowingly.

Dryness of the mouth can also result in a constant chewing motion, as many elderly people do not drink as many fluids as they should. Moving their mouth and jaw can help to stimulate their saliva glands.

Certain tranquilizers and antidepressants can cause a side effect called tardive dyskinesia, a neurological disorder resulting in involuntary body movements of the jaws, mouth, and tongue. It is usually associated with the long-term use of drugs for treating psychotic disorders such as schizophrenia, but a broader spectrum of medicines has also been known to produce the effect.

So, perhaps we shouldn't judge our elderly air chewers too readily—they've probably got a good reason for their constant chewing, and what's more, it's unlikely they even realize they're doing it.

## WHY DOESN'T THE WATER IN FIRE HYDRANTS FREEZE IN THE WINTER?

Used by firefighters to access underground water, the red fire hydrant is a common sight in cities. But in cold climates, why doesn't the water in the hydrants freeze? Could it be because there isn't any water in them to begin with? Well, there is, in some.

In 1801, Frederick Graff, Sr., who was the chief engineer of the Philadelphia Water Works, invented fire hydrants as we see them today. The design, known as the pillar or post type, can either be a wet barrel hydrant or a dry barrel hydrant. Graff developed the wet barrel type, which has the main valve on top, allowing a constant flow of water into the hydrant. These hydrants can only be used in warm climates, because otherwise the water in them will freeze.

In cold climates, the dry barrel hydrant is used because water doesn't always flow into the hydrant. They have two valves, the main valve and the drain valve. Only one valve is open at a time. The main valve allows water to flow into the hydrant while the other helps to drain the water back into the main pipes that are located deep under ground. Unlike the wet barrel hydrant, where the main valve is above ground, the main valve in the dry barrel design is well below ground.

This means that no water remains in the hydrant after use, so there is nothing to freeze. All there is above ground is an empty metallic pipe.

In unusually cold winters, the frost line may move deeper underground and cause damage to the main water pipes, sometimes damaging the hydrant's valves as well. Fire crews are often out testing the hydrants in freezing conditions to ensure there are no problems.

Despite the key difference between the two types of fire hydrant, in most cases, dogs don't discriminate.

## ❓ WHY DO DOCTORS HAVE SUCH MESSY HANDWRITING?

We've all experienced it. You go to the doctor, who gives you a prescription, and when you try to read it, it's completely illegible and looks like something a toddler might have produced. How could anyone possibly make it through medical school with such horrendous handwriting? And how does the pharmacist manage to read it?

The leading theory behind their extraordinary hand-writing is that they're in a hurry, both physically and mentally. Doctors generally have a large workload, and as their patients build up, the quality of their handwriting deteriorates. Before computers became common, doctors were legally required to handwrite a lot of notes documenting the symptoms and treatment for each patient. The time pressure associated with these notes led to messy writing.

Doctors may realize that they are likely the only ones who will have to read their penmanship. Most of the time it will just be the doctor referring to the notes, which will end up filed away, never to see the light of day again. What's the point in writing neatly in these circumstances?

And then there's the more cynical theory. The doctors could hold the belief that they are supposed to have bad handwriting, and so write that way on purpose.

But how do the pharmacists cope? A doctor's handwriting is usually decipherable by others in the profession, because they are familiar with the medical terms and drug names, and so are able to put them into context. They are also more experienced in reading terrible writing, so have developed that skill.

But it's not all a big joke. Court juries are more likely to associate illegible handwriting with substandard medical care in malpractice suits.

## ❓ WHY DON'T BUSES HAVE SEATBELTS?

The first thing you're told when you get into a car as a child is to buckle your seatbelt. It's considered the most important item in car safety, yet buses don't have them. Why?

Because they're safe. Statistically speaking, buses are the safest way to transport school children, up to forty times safer than a car. But what makes buses so safe?

First, it's their size and color. Color makes them very visible and easily identifiable, and their large bulk makes them safer in collisions. Their height affords the driver an excellent view of the road and other cars, making a bus less likely to hit anything, as well as keeping the passengers above the impact height that any car might make.

However, the key safety mechanism is the compart-mentalized structure of the inner bus. The seats are placed very close together, with high backs that are padded with thick foam. The shell of the bus is also reinforced against any impact. These factors give an egg carton effect, securing the entire structure in a protective bubble. As a result, in an accident, a passenger is propelled only a short distance forward into a padded seatback that absorbs most of the impact, like an early version of an airbag.

Financial considerations also govern the lack of seatbelts. The cost of installing numerous belts on every bus would be prohibitive, and belts would also reduce a bus's seating capacity, which would affect profits. In the end, the costs simply outweigh the benefits.

So, is the system working?

Yes. According to annual statistics compiled by the National Highway Traffic Safety Administration, around

440,000 public school buses carry 24 million children more than 4.3 billion miles per year in the US, yet only about six children die on average each year in bus accidents. And most of these fatalities wouldn't have been prevented by a seatbelt, because the passenger's seating position was in direct line with the crash forces. By contrast, about 800 children die on average each year walking, biking, or being driven to school in cars.

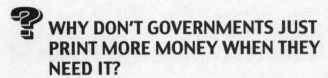

## WHY DON'T GOVERNMENTS JUST PRINT MORE MONEY WHEN THEY NEED IT?

When the economy's bad, national debt is high, and nobody has much money to spend, why doesn't the government simply print more money? They have the machines to do it, and it's unlikely anybody would notice anyway. Or would they?

Yes, they would. Wealth isn't created by money, it's only represented by it. When more money is printed without increasing the wealth it represents, each banknote represents a smaller slice of the financial pie. Economic output is not increased in any way, and all that results is inflation. Using a simplistic example, if an economy produces one million items at $10 each and then doubles the amount of money available by printing it, there will still be only one million items available. The demand for the items will rise. They will then be worth $20 each, and nobody will be any better off because their money has devalued.

Inflation in this situation has many negative impacts:

- The value of savings falls.
- It creates uncertainty and confusion, which discourages companies from investing in the economy. This, in turn, leads to lower economic growth.
- Governments borrow money by selling government bonds to the private sector. As bonds are a form of saving, when inflation rises, the value of bonds decreases. To entice investors, the government would have to increase the return on the bonds and would have more difficulty selling them to reduce the national debt.
- Inflation reduces the value of a currency. If prices double and you need twice as much money to buy the same goods, like in the example on the previous page, the purchasing power of the currency will decline against foreign currencies where the inflation is not as high.

A number of examples throughout history show countries printing money to try to solve their financial problems, most notably Germany in the 1920s. To meet the reparations imposed on them after World War I, the German government printed more money. This led to hyperinflation. Money became worthless and so much was needed to buy goods that some people decided to carry it around in a wheelbarrow. It was said that people would often steal the wheelbarrow, but leave the money. Money was even used as wallpaper. The currency fell to extremely low levels, and the economy collapsed. Printing extra money is not a good idea.

 ## HOW DO FIRE WALKERS DO IT?

Fire walkers have been plying their art for thousands of years, with the world's hottest fire walk in 1997 exceeding 1750°F, a temperature used for cremations. Most fire walkers escape without so much as a blister, and it's nothing to do with any supernatural force or some incredible conjuring of mind over matter. In fact, there's no gimmick to it at all. So, how *do* they walk across a bed of red-hot coals without getting burned?

1. **The right wood.** Hardwoods such as cherry or maple wood are the best, because they're excellent insulators and will protect the feet from some of the heat, despite their embers glowing a daunting orange color.
2. **Prepared coals.** The coals should be raked, as this will spread cooler charcoal to the surface, adding insulation. The coals should also be flattened down to

stop the feet from sinking into them. It is essential to let all the flames die out, so that no new heat is generated.

3. **Ash.** A layer of ash should be sprinkled over the coals. This acts as an insulator, blocking some of the heat from the coals. A fire walk is always done at night so that the orange coals can be seen glowing through the ash. In the daytime, it would just look like a bed of ash—nowhere near as impressive.

4. **Water on the feet.** The walker's feet are dipped in water before the walk. When the liquid meets the intense heat of the coals, it forms an insulating layer of steam, in what's known as the Leidenfrost effect.

5. **Walking, not running.** An expert fire walker will always walk briskly, but never run, and never stop. Running or stopping will concentrate too much weight on the coals, causing the feet to sink in. Walking quickly means that the feet will not sink into the coals as readily. It also means there is not much time to allow the coals to transfer their heat to the feet. Besides, running looks very undignified.

6. **Thermal capacity.** Coal has a low thermal capacity, which means it's a poor conductor and takes a relatively long time for the heat to transfer from the coal to the skin of the feet. In addition, the high blood flow in the feet helps to carry the heat away and dissipate it throughout the body.

So, it looks like there's not much to fire walking after all. Good luck!

## WHAT ARE THE ORIGINS OF THE MEXICAN WAVE?

Known in the United States as simply the wave, the Mexican wave takes place in sporting stadiums around the world when a large crowd acts in unison, with the people standing up in turn and throwing their arms in the air to create the effect of a wave traveling across the group. Just how did this strange pastime begin?

The wave was the brainchild of professional cheerleader "Krazy" George Henderson. At a major league baseball game between the Oakland Athletics and the New York Yankees on October 15, 1981, Krazy George explained to three sections of the crowd what he wanted to happen. The first couple of wave attempts broke down, but after much booing by the rest of the crowd, by the fourth attempt, a continuous wave swept around the entire stadium.

There is, however, a rival claimant. Former *Entertainment Tonight* host, Robb Weller, says that he and Dave Hunter

led the first wave at a football game at the University of Washington's Husky Stadium in Seattle on October 31, 1981. Weller was an alumni cheerleader and Hunter was one of the band's trumpet players. The problem with this claim is that it occurred two weeks after Krazy George's debut, which was recorded for posterity on national television, the announcers even commenting on it. It is generally believed that Weller simply borrowed the idea after seeing Krazy George do it.

That said, the University of Washington certainly helped to popularize the wave, as it was used for all the Huskies' home games in 1981. From there, it spread to other universities, and then to the Detroit Tigers' baseball games in 1984, a season in which they won the World Series, gaining the wave even more national attention. The wave then got a large amount of publicity at the 1984 Los Angeles Olympics, but it wasn't until the 1986 FIFA World Cup in Mexico that the wave received international acclaim. That event earned the wave its longer name.

A 2002 study conducted by Tamás Vicsek at the Eötvös Loránd University in Hungary found that a wave has to be initiated, never occurs spontaneously, and requires a minimum of twenty-five people acting in concert to get going. It also found that waves in the northern hemisphere almost always go clockwise. No comment was made about the direction of southern hemisphere waves.

But whatever your view of the wave, halt one at your peril. If you're at a stadium and you and the people nearby refuse to join in, breaking the wave, you will be met with a barrage of booing and jeering. Wave on.

## ❓ WHAT IS THE DIFFERENCE BETWEEN AN EMU AND AN OSTRICH?

They look very similar, neither can fly, both have big bushy feathers, both can run really fast, and they are the two largest birds in the world, so what is the difference between an emu and an ostrich?

**1. Home.** There is one species of emu, and it is native to Australia. There are five species of ostrich, and they are all native to Africa.

**2. Size and lifespan.** Emus are the second largest bird in the world and stand up to 6 feet tall, weigh up to 132 pounds, and live up to twenty years. Ostriches are the largest bird in the world and are far bigger. They can stand 9 feet tall and weigh up to 320 pounds. They also live up to fifty years.

**3. Appearance.** Emus have deep brown feathers and, unlike with ostriches, it's difficult to

*Ostrich (top) and emu (bottom)*

distinguish between the male and the female. Male ostriches have black feathers with white on the wings and tails, while the females have gray-brown feathers. Ostriches also have much bigger eyes, the largest of any land animal.

**4. Speed.** Both animals have very strong legs and are built for speed. However, the emu has three toes and can run at speeds of up to 30 mph, while ostriches only have two toes, but can run as fast as 40 mph.

**5. Farming.** Emus are farmed for meat, oil, and leather. Ostriches are farmed for feathers, meat, and leather.

**6. Mating.** Emus pair for mating, but the males alone incubate the eggs and raise the chicks. Ostriches form groups, with each male having a harem of up to seven females. The male and female take turns in incubation. Ostrich eggs are white and weigh almost 3 pounds, the largest of any bird, while emu eggs are greenish-blue and weigh about 1 pound.

In the end, while they may seem very similar at a glance, there are actually quite a few differences between these two large, flightless birds.

## WHY DO FIREHOUSES OFTEN HAVE DALMATIANS?

Dalmatians have been depicted as firehouse dogs so often in movies and books that they're practically a stereotype. How did that come about?

The tradition of Dalmatians in firehouses dates back more than a century to a time when they once played a vital role. The English aristocrats of the early 1700s used the dogs to accompany their horse-drawn carriages. The dogs were very adept at keeping pace with the carriages over long distances, and would defend the horses from other dogs or animals. They became a status symbol of sorts, and the more

Dalmatians you had running beside your coach, the higher up the social ladder you appeared to be.

Because of their association with carriages, in the early times of firefighting, when horse-drawn carriages were driven to fires, Dalmatians were employed to run alongside. And they served a number of key purposes.

The dogs were kept in the firehouses, and when the alarm sounded, they would run out barking. This would alert bystanders to clear out of the way so that the carriage could easily exit. The dogs would then run alongside the carriage, scaring away anything that might spook the horses and barking to alert pedestrians to move out of the way. Once at the fire, the dogs provided comfort to the horses, who were generally afraid of fire, and also stood guard at the wagon, ensuring that nobody stole the firefighters' belongings, equipment, or even the horses themselves.

With the advent of the fire truck, you would think that Dalmatians would no longer be needed, but many firehouses have kept the dogs around to preserve the tradition. They have turned into firehouse mascots, particularly popular

when firefighters go around teaching children about fire safety. And the dogs still protect the firefighters' possessions, but these days they ride inside the trucks instead of running alongside.

## ❓ IS LAUGHTER REALLY THE BEST MEDICINE?

Everyone enjoys a good laugh from time to time, but is it really the best medicine like many people claim? Can it actually improve your health?

It seems so. The benefits of laughter are many and varied.

1. **Relaxing the body.** This relieves physical tension in the muscles, stimulates circulation, and thereby reduces stress.

2. **Boosting the immune system.** Laughter does this by decreasing stress hormones and increasing the release of neuropeptides, a chemical that helps fight stress and improve your resistance to disease.

3. **Triggering the release of endorphins.** This promotes an overall sense of well-being and can even temporarily relieve pain.

4. **Protecting the heart.** By increasing blood flow, laughter improves the function of blood vessels and helps protect against cardiovascular problems. It also enhances the intake of oxygen-rich air, which stimulates the heart, lungs, and other muscles.

5. **Burning calories.** This improves overall well-being.

6. **Strengthening relationships.** This can have a profound effect on mental and emotional health.

All of this is easy to say, but has any of it been proven?

In a 2014 study conducted at California's Loma Linda University, researchers assessed the short-term memory and stress levels of twenty adults in their sixties and seventies. One group sat silently while the other watched funny videos. The participants then took a memory test. Those who'd watched the funny videos performed significantly better, at 43.6 percent compared with 20.3 percent in the non-humor group. Saliva samples also showed that the humor group had considerably lower levels of the stress hormone cortisol.

Another 2011 study from the University of Oxford tested the impact that laughter had on the pain threshold of volunteers. One group was shown comedy videos while the other was shown boring videos. The comedy video subjects were then able to withstand up to 10 percent more pain than they had done before watching the videos. The boring video subjects were able to bear less pain than before. Professor Robin Dunbar, who led the research, said the type of laughter is important. In order to release the pain-relieving endorphins, a strong belly laugh is required, as opposed to simply tittering or giggling, which has little effect.

In addition to benefiting the body physically, laughter also makes you feel good and improves your mood, increasing positivity and optimism, as well as reducing depression and anxiety. In fact, some experts believe that the physical act of laughing is what is needed, and that simulated laughter can be just as beneficial as the real thing.

So, whether you're faking it or not, it's no joke, laughter really might be the best medicine.

# ? WHAT DO MOSQUITOES DO DURING THE DAY?

Mosquitoes are a bane for anyone who steps outside from dusk to dawn. But during the day, you're free to wander around without a thought for the bloodthirsty little cretins. This leads some people to ask, where do mosquitoes go during the daytime?

First, only the female mosquitoes bite. They suck blood in order to obtain protein to develop their eggs. For nutritional purposes, both the males and females primarily feed on the nectar from plants. All of this feeding occurs while the sun is down. Why?

They feed while it's dark for survival reasons. Mosquitoes don't like the hot, dry sun, which can dehydrate and kill them. They also don't like wind, which requires a lot of energy to fly into. During the night, it is usually less hot and windy, so that's when they come out.

During the heat of the day, most mosquitoes seek shade and darkness in densely wooded areas that also hold more moisture. There, they are able to sleep, protected from the wind and the heat. The more humidity the better, so they often tuck into vegetation, such as plants or grass. They also rest in caves, holes in the ground, hollow logs, or holes in trees. When it comes to man-made structures, they sleep in any dark place where they're unlikely to be disturbed, such as basements, closets, in curtains, or under beds.

But just because you don't see them in the day doesn't mean they're not there, waiting patiently to strike.

## ❓ WHY DOES FIRE MAKE A CRACKLING SOUND?

If you love the great outdoors, you probably love nothing more than sitting around an open campfire, watching the flames and listening to the crackling sound. Have you ever wondered why fires snap and crackle like popcorn cooking?

When you put a log of wood onto a fire, it begins to burn. Wood contains tiny pockets of fluids, such as sap and water. As the wood burns, the fire heats these fluids, causing them to boil and then vaporize into steam. As it heats, the steam expands, trapped inside the pockets within the wood. This expanding steam begins to exert pressure on the surrounding wood, until the wood gives way and cracks open. The crackling noise that you hear is the wood splitting along a crevice as the steam escapes.

Different woods make more of a crackling sound than others. Softwoods, like hemlock, pine, cedar, and spruce, contain large amounts of resin and pockets of moisture, so they tend to make a lot of noise. Some hardwoods, such as sumac, black locust, and sassafras, also contain moisture and crackle a lot when burned.

This phenomenon is most noticeable if wet or green wood is burned. Because of the excess water and sap that is trapped within the wood, it will generally snap, crackle, and pop like a bowl of breakfast cereal.

# WHY ISN'T THERE A LIGHT IN THE FREEZER, BUT ONE IN THE FRIDGE?

After reading this question, you're probably now carrying this book over to your refrigerator to check if the freezer compartment has a light in it or not. It's not something a lot of people think about on a daily basis. But now that you've had a look, chances are you've discovered there is no light in there. Why not, as there's one in the fridge section?

This domestic anomaly can be explained by the following theories:

1. The freezer is usually densely packed, much more so than the fridge, and it's sometimes coated with ice. A light would be obstructed and would not provide much illumination.

2. The freezer doesn't get opened anywhere near as often as the fridge, and when people open the freezer, they know exactly what they're going for, so there's not as much browsing.

3. People go to the fridge at night for a snack without turning on the kitchen light. This rarely happens with the freezer; when the freezer is opened, it's usually either daytime or the kitchen light is on anyway.

4. Fresh food in the fridge looks tastier when it's lit up, whereas in the freezer, a pizza box is a pizza box, so it doesn't need to look as appealing.

5. A lot of freezers have pull-out drawers, which means that a light would be required for each drawer, and the placement of those lights would be awkward.  Plus, the drawers are pulled out into the light of the room, which then illuminates them sufficiently.

6. The old-style incandescent lights could potentially shatter with the constant heating and cooling as they go on and off.

7. It costs money to install another light that isn't strictly necessary, and manufacturers are always trying to save as much money as they can. A lot of high-end units do have a light in both the fridge and the freezer sections, supporting this theory.

## DON'T POLICE SIRENS ALERT THE BAD GUYS THAT THE COPS ARE ON THEIR WAY?

Picture the scene: You've got the balaclava on, the customers are lying on the ground, you've controlled the bank staff well, their hands are in the air, and you're sure nobody's hit the panic button. Most of the money is in the bags, but you've got all the time in the world so you keep stuffing it in there. Suddenly, you hear the sirens. No! Someone must have called the cops. Luckily, you can hear the sirens in the distance so there's now time to escape. If they hadn't put those sirens on, you could have been in all sorts of trouble. Why on earth did they give the game away like that?

The main reason why police use their sirens is to get to the scene safely and without harm to others. A siren alerts other motorists and tells them to make way for a fast-moving vehicle. It also warns pedestrians to keep clear. In addition, a police car does not technically become an emergency vehicle until both its lights and siren are activated. Until that time, the officer is bound by all applicable traffic rules and can't lawfully violate stop signs and red lights. If a crash occurs while the lights and sirens are on, the officer's liability is far more likely to be reduced.

But whether the siren is sounded or not often depends on the situation. For example:

- In most robberies, the suspect has already gone by the time the police are notified, so the siren helps them get to the scene faster.

- Alerting the suspect by using the siren can assist police, as the siren can prompt a fleeing suspect to hide as opposed to running. This can give the police a chance to establish a perimeter and trap a suspect, later flushing the suspect out with dogs.

- If a violent assault is in progress, the use of the siren may cause the assailant to break off the attack and flee earlier than they would have otherwise. In many cases, this could save a victim's life.

- Hearing the siren may decrease an attacker's morale while increasing the confidence of any police at the scene, giving the police an edge.
- In cases where a burglary is in process and it's unlikely anyone will be injured, the police often turn their sirens off a few minutes before arriving in the hope of retaining the element of surprise and apprehending the suspect.

In the end, it depends on the circumstances, and the use of the siren is all a matter of balancing the safety considerations with the tactical benefits.

## ❓ CAN ONE SPIDER GET CAUGHT IN THE WEB OF ANOTHER?

If you've ever accidentally run into a spider's web, you know just how sticky they are and how difficult it is to get all the web off. A spider's silk is indeed very sticky, and it's also very strong. These two elements combined make a spider's web

perfect for catching prey, like flies, bees, and moths. But what about other spiders? Do they get stuck too?

A spider uses different glands to produce different types of silk. Sticky silk is designed to catch insects, while stronger, nonsticky silk is used to tie down the web and for its frame. When making a web, a spider will use nonsticky silk to make the web frame and the threads that run out from the center. This is because the spider needs to walk along the structure to weave the rest of the web and to traverse the web generally. A spider's legs are also covered in an oily coating that helps to prevent it from getting stuck in its own web. In addition, they regularly groom themselves to remove any excess silk or other debris that might cause them to get stuck.

The problem for other spiders is that, like insects, they may not see the web and may not know which parts of it are sticky or not. If it is the same type of web that the other spider regularly weaves, it will be familiar with the web and unlikely to get caught in it. However, a different variety of spider is likely to have more difficulty. The portia spider actually builds a web that attaches to the webs of other spiders, so that the prey spider mistakes the predator spider's web for a portion of its own and often becomes entangled. Cellar spiders (also called daddy longlegs) are similarly known to prey on other spiders, such as brown recluses, black widows, and wolf spiders.

So, other spiders do often get caught in webs, and when they do, spiders generally have no qualms about committing acts of cannibalism—the hapless victim becomes a meal just like anything else.

## ❓ HOW DO AUTHORITIES MARK BANKNOTES?

If you ever find yourself in the dubious position of collecting a ransom payment, how can you tell if the banknotes are marked, and what does that even mean?

Police mark bills to trace and identify money used in illegal activities. They do this in two ways:

1. **Physical marking.** Traditionally, bills were marked physically with a pen or stamp mark that could be seen. As technology developed, invisible ink was used, which could only be seen under ultraviolet light. An alert is put out to financial institutions to be aware of such bills and to notify the authorities if one is seen. Banks are sometimes asked to try to keep the person who gave the bill in the bank for as long as possible until the authorities arrive to question them.

2. **Serial numbers.** Recording serial numbers is probably the most common way to "mark" bills these days. If a criminal is caught with cash, those bills are then checked against a list of marked serial numbers, which could be useful in solving a prior case where the marked bills were used. The serial numbers are also entered into a database, so if someone makes a deposit at a bank, the bank can use a machine to scan the serial numbers while the money is being counted.

In an attempt to get around these two law enforcement techniques, criminals may carry a UV light to see if the bills have been physically marked. However, criminals have no way of telling when the serial numbers of bills have been recorded, since this doesn't affect the physical bill in any way. This is why criminals often ask for the cash in nonsequential bills. This makes it far more difficult for the authorities, because the bills' serial numbers have to be recorded one by one instead of using a range, such as bills numbered 005000 to 006500.

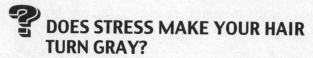

## DOES STRESS MAKE YOUR HAIR TURN GRAY?

Legend has it that Marie Antoinette's hair turned gray on the day she was to be guillotined. And a before-and-after photo of every recent US president has shown their hair color change from dark to gray during their time in office. Was the stress of impending decapitation (literal for Marie and figurative for the presidents) the actual cause of these follicle misfortunes, or is this merely an old wives' tale?

Cells known as keratinocytes build the keratin that becomes our hair, but before it emerges from the follicle, cells known as melanocytes inject a pigment called melanin into the hair, which gives it its color. When our hair turns gray, it's because less melanin is produced. But does stress impact this melanin production?

Many experts say that there is no direct link between stress and gray hair, and if you want to know if you're going to go gray, look at your relatives, because gray hair is up to genetics. Others, however, have different views.

One theory is that gray hair could be the result of chronic free radical damage. Stress hormones may produce inflammation that drives the production of free radicals, which are unstable molecules that damage cells. This, in turn, inhibits the production of melanin by interfering with the signals instructing melanocytes to deliver the melanin pigment. Without the pigment, the hair is gray.

A 2013 study led by Dr. Mayumo Ito from New York University posits another theory. Tests of mice showed that when the skin was damaged elsewhere, a stress hormone called adrenocorticotropic (ACTH) was produced. This ACTH promoted the melanocyte stem cells to migrate from the hair follicle to help repair the damaged skin, leaving the follicle with no capacity to produce melanin. This resulted in the hair turning white. The researchers believe that a similar mechanism could be at play with stress-related graying in humans.

So, what did happen to Marie Antoinette's hair? One of three things, depending on which theory you believe:

1. The stress of her impending doom generated a swarm of free radicals that destroyed the production of melanin in her hair.

2. In a blind panic, her body produced copious amounts of ACTH, which caused all the melanocyte stem cells in her follicles to migrate elsewhere.

3. She decided there was little point in persisting with her vanity and simply removed her wig.

# ❓ WHY WERE DUELS ALWAYS FOUGHT AT DAWN?

It's so common in Western movies that it's almost become a cliché. One guy insults another guy, and the next thing you know, they're facing off with pistols at dawn. But why wait until the next morning? Why not just get on with it?

While duels were fought at other times of the day, dawn was the preferred time for a number of reasons.

* With the sun low in the sky, neither man's vision was hampered by the glaring light. During the day, the sun would be more likely to be behind one of the men, making it far more difficult for the opponent.

* Dueling at dawn ensured privacy and made it less likely that any law enforcement officers would be awake to prevent the duel or arrest the participants.

* Dueling at night was impractical because it would generally be too hard for the men to see each other. Added to that, a lot of men would have been drunk at

night when the argument giving rise to the duel took place. Waiting until dawn forced an interval, allowing the men time to reconsider or sober up and call it off.

Dueling became such a serious pastime during the 18th century that in 1777, a group of Irish gentlemen drew up a set of dueling rules in a document called the *Code Duello*. This code was adopted throughout Ireland before spreading to England, Europe, and America, with only slight variations. The code contained twenty-six specific rules that lean toward dueling at dawn. Rule 15 stated: "Challenges are never to be delivered at night, unless the party to be challenged intends leaving the place of offense before morning; for it is desirable to avoid all hot-headed proceedings." Rule 17 stated: "The challenged chooses his ground; the challenger chooses his distance; the seconds fix the time and terms of firing."

In 1838, former governor of South Carolina John Lyde Wilson published an American version of the code, called *The Code of Honor; or Rules for the Government of Principals and Seconds in Dueling*. While this code merely specified that "the time must be as soon as practicable," the tradition of dueling at dawn persisted.

## ❓ WHY DO PIRATES LOVE PARROTS?

The depiction of pirates with parrots perched on their shoulders stems from the character of Long John Silver in Robert Louis Stevenson's 1883 novel, *Treasure Island*. Stevenson admitted that he got the idea from Daniel Defoe's ground-breaking 1719 work, *Robinson Crusoe*, in which the stranded narrator captures a parrot and keeps it as a pet, but *Treasure Island* popularized the concept. Ever since that time, the pop culture conception of pirates has involved parrots. But that's fiction. Was it ever the case in fact?

Yes, according to Colin Woodard, author of the 2008 book, *The Republic of Pirates: Being the True and Surprising Story of the Caribbean Pirates and the Man Who Brought Them Down.* "The parrot trope is almost certainly grounded in reality," Woodard claims. But how? And why?

During the Golden Age of Piracy in the 17th and 18th centuries, pirates sailed throughout the Atlantic Ocean pillaging anyone they came across. They generally followed the trade routes, often making stops in the Caribbean and Central America, where parrot populations were large. The exotic pet trade in Europe, especially in London and Paris, was booming at the time, with rich people paying a lot of money for unusual animals. The pirates knew this, and when they saw these colorful birds, the only color they really saw was gold. They bought or stole the birds from market vendors and transported them back to the civilized world for sale. Parrots and parrot cages have been found listed among the inventory of ships from that time.

While the birds were shipped more often than they were kept as personal pets, they did provide the added bonus of enjoyable companionship while aboard. The pirates undertook long and boring voyages, and exotic pets provided an interesting distraction. Monkeys were fairly common as well. Parrots had the advantage of being intelligent, eating seeds that could be easily stored, having bright and colorful plumage, and mimicking sounds to entertain the pirates and impress onlookers when in port. Because of these factors, it is likely that a number of parrots were actually kept by the pirates rather than sold.

## WHY DOES WARM MILK HELP PEOPLE SLEEP?

Insomnia? Tossing and turning all night and can't go to sleep? Drinking a cup of warm milk is one of the most common remedies. But is this just another old wives' tale, or is warm milk really the answer to those restless nights of frustration?

The common thought is that milk can help people fall asleep because it contains tryptophan. Tryptophan is an essential amino acid that is not produced by humans but needs to be ingested from foods. It is a precursor for the neurotransmitter serotonin, which gets converted into the hormone melatonin. Known as the "hormone of darkness," melatonin is a sleep-inducing hormone that promotes sleep, either directly or as a time-cue marker that initiates the normal physiological processes that lead to sleep.

However, experts believe that the tryptophan content in a glass of milk is far lower than that contained in a melatonin supplement, and that the dose is most likely too low to have any affect. A lot of other foods contain tryptophan, including chicken, beef, pork, turkey, eggs, and bananas, but also in small amounts.

But even after discounting the physical effects of tryptophan, a number of sleep experts still believe that milk, especially warm milk, does help people sleep. The reason? Psychology. Many people find drinking a warm glass of milk a calming ritual that helps them wind down to sleep. The routine of drinking the milk at night may elicit memories of childhood and comfort, and this may induce sleep by making us relax. Humans like predictability, so the brain recognizes the act of routinely drinking a glass of warm milk each night before bed as behavior that is preparatory to sleep, and this actually makes us sleepy.

## ARE EXTRA-LARGE HENS NEEDED TO LAY EXTRA-LARGE EGGS?

If you go to the grocery store, you'll see that eggs come in a lot of different sizes, from small to medium, all the way up to extra-large. What sort of chicken lays the extra-large eggs? Does it have to be an extra-large hen?

Extra-large eggs generally fetch a higher price per pound than smaller eggs, so the prudent chicken farmer encourages hens to lay big eggs. A number of factors determine egg size.

1. **Age.** The biggest variable in egg size is the age of the chicken. As a rule, the older the chicken, the larger the egg. Hens that lay eggs prematurely usually lay more eggs, but they are smaller.

2. **Weight.** The weight of the chicken is another key factor in egg size. The larger the hen, the larger the egg, so farmers pay particular attention to both the quantity and quality of food provided to the chickens.

3. **Diet.** Chickens that are fed sufficient protein and fatty amino acids tend to produce larger eggs.

4. **Conditions.** Many experts believe that the hatching environment also plays a large role in egg size. Heat, stress, and overcrowded conditions all lower the size of eggs. Conversely, backyard hens usually lay large eggs.

5. **Breed.** Different breeds lay different-sized eggs. The Single-Comb White Leghorn, the most popular laying hen in the United States, tends to lay larger-than-average eggs.

While extra-large and extra-old hens will generally lay extra-large eggs, it does vary, with even those hens laying the occasional medium or small egg. But whatever the size of the eggs, just make sure you don't put them all in one basket.

## ❓ WHAT IS THE HISTORY OF THE SAMURAI?

A Japanese fighting machine, adorned in elaborate armor and wielding a large sword to devastating effect, destroying all who come before him. That's how the samurai warrior is depicted in fiction, but is that what he was really like, and how did the samurai originate?

The samurai tradition began in the 9th century and rose out of the long-term battles for land in Japan among three major clans: the Fujiwara, the Taira, and the Minamoto. Also known as *bushi*, meaning warriors, the samurai were highly trained officers in military tactics and strategy, each associated with a particular clan and landowning lord to whom they pledged their eternal loyalty. The feudal landowners, called *daimyo*, had grown independent of the central government and used their samurai to protect their land and to expand their holdings and power.

In 1185, the Minamoto family took control of Japan after defeating the Taira clan in the Gempei War. Minamoto no Yoritomo became the supreme military commander, or *shogun*, of the country. By this time, the samurai had become an essential part of the military, forming a class of their own, and dominating Japan for the next 700 years. Fighting for land continued between the various factions throughout this time, and these warriors were in high demand.

The samurai became experts in fighting from horseback, and later on foot, and wore extensive armor that included a helmet that protected the head and neck, a breastplate, arm and shoulder protectors, a belly wrap, and leg shields. They employed a range of weapons, from bows and arrows to spears and guns, but their primary weapon was the sword, which became the symbol for which they were known.

The samurai wore two swords that were used for close-in fighting and beheading their enemies. The long sword (*daito-katana*) was more than 24 inches long, while the short sword (*shoto-wakizashi*) was between 12 and 24 inches. The swords had a curved blade and were crafted by highly skilled swordsmiths. The blades were tested by cutting through the bodies of corpses or condemned criminals. The samurai often gave names to their swords, which they believed were the soul of their warriorship.

If the swords were the soul, the strict code that the samurai lived by was the heart. They led their lives according to the ethics of *bushido*, the way of the warrior. Strongly Confucian in nature, it stressed principles such as self-discipline, respect, ethics, and complete loyalty to one's master. One of the key philosophies of bushido was freedom from fear. This meant that the samurai transcended his fear of death, giving him the peace and power to faithfully serve his master, dying with honor if necessary. The  samurai were also known to practice Zen Buddhism and meditation to ground them and fortify their beliefs. Breaches of the bushido code were rare.

Japan was reunited in the late 1500s, and a rigid social caste system established, with the samurai at the top. They lived in castle towns, were the only people allowed to own and carry swords, and were paid by the daimyo in rice. Masterless samurai, called ronin, roamed the land, and were effectively freelance mercenaries.

Over the next 250 years, Japan remained in relative peace, and the importance of expert martial skills declined. In 1868, a new government was empowered and the feudal era came to an end. The daimyo were forced to return their lands to the emperor Meiji, who was moved from Kyoto to Tokyo, which became the new capital. In 1876, Meiji outlawed the wearing of swords, and the samurai class was abolished after almost 1,000 years of dominance.

While the samurai numbered less than 10 percent of Japan's population, their teachings can still be found in everyday Japanese life, and their legend and mystique live on around the world.

 ## JUST HOW SAFE IS FORT KNOX?

Fort Knox is a US Army post south of Louisville in Kentucky. Used in various capacities as a military facility, it is best known as the site of the United States Bullion Depository. It houses a large portion of the country's gold reserves, estimated as 2.3 percent of all the gold ever refined throughout human history—over 4,500 metric tons, valued at more than $180 billion. Frequently referenced in popular culture, from criminal plots in James Bond to comedy routines by Abbott and Costello, the Depository has also housed other valuables over the years, including the original Declaration of Independence, as well as large supplies of morphine and opium during World War II. It has become a symbol of the ultimate impregnable vault and has given rise to the phrase "as safe as Fort Knox." But is that expression correct? Just how safe is Fort Knox?

The Depository, often itself known as Fort Knox, is a fortified vault. In 1933, President Franklin D. Roosevelt issued an order outlawing the private ownership of gold coins. This led to a vast increase in the gold held by the Federal Reserve, which needed a place to store it. As a result, the facility was constructed in 1936, with the gold vault alone costing $560,000 to build (around $10 million in today's terms).

The gold vault is lined with granite walls and protected by a 21-inch-thick blast-proof door that weighs 20 tons. This door, as well as another 21-inch-thick inner emergency door, is made of torch- and drill-resistant material. The vault casing is 25 inches thick. To enter the vault, members of the depository staff must dial separate combinations known only to them. There is an escape tunnel from the lower level of the vault in case someone is accidentally locked in.

The facility itself is ringed with electric fences and guarded by the heavily armed United States Mint Police, as well as 30,000 Fort Knox army personnel and their associated artillery, tanks, and attack helicopters. No visitors are allowed inside the depository grounds, which are further protected by alarms, video cameras, microphones, barbed razor wire, and mine fields.

So, just how safe is Fort Knox? Pretty safe.

## IS THERE A FINE LINE BETWEEN PLEASURE AND PAIN?

The Divinyls sang about it, but it's not just pop bands who've made the link. Philosophers from Aristotle to Descartes to Jeremy Bentham have been hypothesizing about the connection between pleasure and pain for centuries. Is there any basis for this, or is it just a catchy thing to say?

There is strong evidence of the biological connection between the neurochemical pathways used for the perception of both pleasure and pain. Both feelings originate from neurons in the same locations of the brain: the amygdala, the pallidum, and the nucleus accumbens. A functional relationship between pleasure and pain also exists, in that pain itself elicits analgesia, which is the relief from pain, effectively a form of pleasure. In a 1999 study conducted at the University of California,

San Francisco, researchers found that in response to pain, the reward pathways of the brain activate pain relief through the release of opioids, a morphine-like drug produced by the body, and dopamine, a chemical whose effects can be mimicked by cocaine or amphetamines. It had been previously thought that the release of dopamine was only associated with positive experiences, but the study, done on rats, showed that pain and its relief (pleasure) are actually linked. This can potentially explain why a painful stimulus that activates the release of opioids and dopamine may actually be experienced as rewarding, as appears to occur in people who exhibit self-injurious behavior.

Scientists have prophesized that the relationship between the two perceptions likely provided an evolutionary advantage. The brain is limited, and for efficiency, tends to focus on its most frequently used pathways. Having a common pathway for both pleasure and pain could have simplified the way in which our ancestors interacted with the environment in order to best survive. The link may have made it easier to weigh a variety of decisions. For example, a person may have been willing to endure a small amount of pain in order to obtain a large reward of pleasure-inducing food. When a decision such as that is governed by the one pathway, a more coherent and beneficial answer would have been likely, leading to a greater chance of survival.

## HOW DID THE STRANGE SCORING SYSTEM IN TENNIS COME ABOUT?

15-0, 15-30, 30-30, 40-30—not even Einstein would have been able to calculate the next set of numbers in that progression. And then they say "love" for 0. How *did* the arcane tennis scoring system originate?

**Love**—One theory of love's origin is that at the start of each game, when the scores are at zero, the players still have love for each other.

Another is that it comes from the Dutch expression *iets voor lof doen*, meaning something done for praise, with no money at stake.

These two explanations are unlikely, however, and most tennis historians believe that it comes from the French word *l'oeuf*, meaning the egg, because an egg looks like the number zero. Over the years, the pronunciation of the French word was altered until it became love.

**15-30-40**—Three possibilities explain the use of 15, 30, and 40 in tennis. Nobody knows which is correct, and all seem equally meritorious.

It is thought that clock faces might have been used on court, with a quarter move of the hand to indicate the scores of 15, 30, and 45. When the hand moved to 60, the game was won. However, to ensure that the game could not be won by only one point, the idea of *deuce* was introduced, meaning two, or that both players were equal. To make the score stay within the clock face's 60, the 45 was changed to 40. This allowed another two points to be easily divided. If both players were at 40, or deuce, the next score moved the player to 50 (now "advantage"), and another point took the player to 60 to win the game. Opponents of this theory say that clocks in medieval times, when the scoring system was developed, only recorded the hours from 1 to 12 and did not have minute hands.

A similar theory involves the use of a circle. Medieval Europeans were interested in astronomy and geometry. In early records of the game in France, sets were played to four or six games. A sextant, being one-sixth of a circle, was 60 degrees, so each point was worth 15 degrees, making a game 60 degrees. By winning six games, a player had completed a full circle of 360 degrees, and so had won the set. The 45

may have later been changed to 40 for the same reason in the clock theory.

The final theory is that the scoring system came from the French game *jeu de paume*, a precursor to tennis that used the hand instead of a racket. This game was very popular before the French Revolution, with more than 1,000 courts in Paris alone. The court was 90 feet long, 45 feet on each side of the net. Upon scoring, the server got to move up 15 feet, then another 15 feet if another point was scored. Since a third score would put the server right at the net, 10 feet was the last move forward, giving the scores of 15, 30, and 40.

## WHY DO CATS MARCH UP AND DOWN ON CARPET?

Domestic cats display a common behavior: They march up and down on one spot, pushing forward with their paws as they alternate between left and right. This is known as kneading, because the motion resembles a baker kneading dough, but is there any point to this mysterious behavioral quirk?

It is unclear why cats knead, but a number of hypotheses exist.

1. Kneading is a behavior that has persisted since kittenhood. A kitten will knead the area around its mother's teat to stimulate milk flow. It is thought that an adult cat will knead when it's feeling content because it associates the motion with the security of its mother and the comforts it experienced as a kitten. Adding weight to this theory is the fact that cats often

purr when they're kneading and will sometimes even suckle on the surface they're kneading.

2. Kneading was done by cats in a time before domestication in order to pat down grass or foliage to make a soft and comfortable surface for sleeping or to give birth. The behavior may persist today because it's become an instinctual part of a cat preparing for rest.

3. Cats have scent glands in their paws, so some believe that kneading is a way for them to scent and stake a claim to an area. This may have served as a territorial marker to ward off unfamiliar cats.

Whatever the reason they do it, a cat should never be punished for kneading, as it's a natural and instinctive activity that means the cat is content. If a cat kneads you, try to ignore the pain of the claws digging into your lap. It's a form of feline flattery, and indicates that the cat is feeling comfortable and secure, and perhaps marking you as its own.

## WHY ARE THE CEILINGS IN TRAIN STATIONS SO HIGH?

If you're a daily train user, you know that the journeys can be long and monotonous, and at times your mind may wander to the minutiae of life. And, being in train stations a lot, one of the questions you ask yourself may well be, why are the ceilings so high?

Some say the high ceilings enable the boards with the train times to be raised so that they're easy to see above the people's heads. Others claim they are high to allow more natural light in, and any hot air to rise up high and make the station cooler. Along with lower and upper windows, this produces a flow of air to further cool things down. Train aficionados often claim that the ceilings were made high because the stations were built at a time when the train was king. A large and impressive station gave a sense of grandeur and prestige and was often the first thing people saw when they arrived at a city.

While these ideas sound feasible and may have played a minor role in the high ceilings, the actual reason is that the stations were built in the days of steam engines. The trains emitted a great deal of pollution, yet the stations needed a roof to shelter the waiting passengers from the elements. The solution was to make the ceilings very high. The hot steam drifted upward and away from the passengers. Had the ceilings been low, the stations would have been filled with a dense fog of steam, making conditions hot and uncomfortable, as well as reducing visibility markedly.

## ❓ DO GLASSES WEAKEN YOUR EYES?

The vast majority of people need glasses at some point in their lives to correct their vision, whether it's due to far-sightedness (hyperopia), short-sightedness (myopia), or any other eye condition. Glasses are designed to correct the specific condition, yet there is a commonly held belief that wearing glasses too often will weaken your eyes and actually make things worse. Is there any basis to this?

Put simply, no. Glasses don't change the process of any eye condition.

The erroneous belief is based on the idea that wearing glasses makes your eyes lazy. Your eyes grow accustomed to wearing glasses, so that once you remove them, you can't see as well as before.

Glasses work to correct your vision, which means your eye muscles can relax and work naturally. But when the glasses are removed, the muscles that bend and straighten the lens of your eye must suddenly work harder than normal to make your eyes focus. This can make your vision blurry and make you feel disorientated or dizzy. However, your eyes will get used to working harder again and will adjust back. They won't be worse than before as a result of wearing the glasses.

Another reason people think that glasses increase eye deterioration is because when you're wearing them you can see clearly, so when you take them off, the contrasting blurriness is far more noticeable. In addition, most people's eyes are more flexible first thing in the morning, before they put their glasses on, and they are better at focusing than they are later in the day, when they take their glasses off. This leads some to believe that the glasses are responsible for making their vision worse.

The most probable reason behind the myth, however, is that vision generally deteriorates with age, regardless of whether you wear glasses or not. People who wear glasses for years discover that their eyes are not as good over time, but this is likely caused by the aging process rather than the glasses themselves. When wearers find that they need their glasses more often, they think that the glasses have made their sight worse, when in reality, there's no causal link.

Strangely, however, virtually no studies on the topic have been conducted. Professor Ananth Viswanathan from the Moorfields Eye Hospital in London believes the lack of research is due to the absence of any genuine physiological reason why glasses might damage eyesight.

So, while there may be many reasons to choose not to wear glasses, the fear that you're damaging your eyesight shouldn't be one of them. On the other side of the coin, glasses won't cure your poor vision either.

## WHY DO FISH FLOAT UPSIDE DOWN WHEN THEY DIE?

Few things in childhood are more traumatizing (and in retrospect, more predictable), than waking up one morning to find your beloved pet fish floating upside down in the tank. While it's certainly a horrible experience that many of us have endured and don't want to live through again, the question is still worth asking: What's the reason for the morbid buoyancy of our scaly friends?

Fish are neutrally buoyant, which means it takes little effort for a fish to sink. This is because fish are only slightly denser than water, so the force of the water pushing them up and down is practically equal. However, when a fish swims deeper, the pressure increases. To maintain its neutral buoyancy and stay in that position, the fish relies on an internal organ called a swim bladder. The swim bladder works to counteract the difference in pressure. When water enters a fish's mouth, its gills extract oxygen and some of it is released into the swim bladder to regulate the fish's depth. The more oxygen released into the bladder, the more the fish will float upward, and vice versa.

When a fish dies, oxygen remains in the swim bladder, and as the fish's body decomposes, additional gases also begin to fill the bladder. After it is dead, the fish is unable to empty its  bladder, causing it to float to the surface. As most of a fish's mass is in the bone and muscle in its back, just underneath the buoyant bladder, the fish is likely to hydrostatically roll, or in simple terms, go belly up. This is also why injured or sick fish will sometimes swim on their side; they lose the ability to maintain their equilibrium and the more buoyant part of their body forces its way to the surface.

Sometimes a fish will sink when it dies, and later float. This is because the fish has died with very little oxygen in its bladder, so the weight of the fish makes it sink. The decomposition process then begins and generally produces enough gas to cause the fish to float to the surface.

## ❓ IS BREAKFAST REALLY THE MOST IMPORTANT MEAL OF THE DAY?

For generations, people have been told that breakfast is the most important meal of the day. Breakfast like a king, lunch like a prince, and dine like a pauper, as the saying goes. But this mandate has been brought into question in recent times, creating a nutritional controversy. So, is breakfast the cornerstone of a healthy diet, or is it an optional morning meal?

**Does skipping breakfast make you fatter?** While skipping breakfast may make people eat more for lunch, studies have shown that it results in a lower calorie intake over the course of the day. A 2013 study conducted at Cornell University found that college students ate about 145 calories more at lunch when they skipped breakfast, but given that their breakfasts averaged 625 calories, this resulted in a daily saving of 450 calories, as their evening meal usually remained the same regardless of whether breakfast was eaten or not. Another study from the University of Alabama found no difference after sixteen weeks in weight loss between people

who were randomly assigned to eat breakfast and people who were randomly assigned to skip it. Despite the common association between skipping breakfast and weight gain, there is no evidence to support this.

**Does breakfast kick-start your metabolism?** It has long been said that eating breakfast sets a variety of biological processes associated with digestion into motion; that is, breakfast kick-starts your metabolism and makes you lose weight as a result. A 2014 study from the University of Bath in England looked at this issue by monitoring 33 volunteers, some who ate breakfast and some who didn't. After six weeks, the resting metabolic rates, cholesterol levels, and blood sugar levels of the subjects were largely unchanged. However, the breakfast-eaters burned around 500 more calories per day in physical activity, but also ate an additional 500 calories each day. So, while eating breakfast provided more energy, the net caloric effect was the same.

**Does eating breakfast make you smarter?** There is evidence to support the fact that eating breakfast is important for brain development in growing children. In a 2013 study of a group of Chinese kindergarten students that was published in the Elsevier journal *Early Human Development*, it was found that those who regularly ate breakfast had higher IQ scores than those who didn't. These results held even after accounting for other factors, such as their parents' occupations and education.

**Does eating breakfast keep the doctor away?** A number of 2012 and 2013 studies reported in the *American Journal of Clinical Nutrition* and in *Circulation* found that breakfast-eaters had a lower risk of type 2 diabetes, as well as heart disease. Further study is needed to substantiate these findings, but they do suggest that eating breakfast is beneficial to well-being.

***

The bottom line? Nobody is quite sure. Eating breakfast is unlikely to make you lose weight; however, it may make you inclined to do more exercise but at the same time eat more calories. It may help prevent certain diseases, and it may make your kids smarter. But if you don't like eating breakfast, the scientific evidence that we currently have indicates that you can feel more justified in skipping it.

## ❓ HOW DISASTROUS WOULD THE EXTINCTION OF BEES REALLY BE?

Bees can be an annoyance. They buzz around, land in our drinks, chase us down the street, and even sting us. For some people who are allergic, they can be a lethal threat. Yet some experts claim that if bees didn't exist, humans wouldn't exist. Albert Einstein once said that "mankind will not survive the honeybees' disappearance for more than five years." Is there any basis to these grave allegations? Where would we be without bees?

Probably still here, but much, much hungrier.

Bees collect pollen from plants as a source of protein for their hives and offspring. In the process, a dusting of pollen clings to the hairs on the bee's body and is transferred to other plants, pollinating them and ensuring the next generation.

This pollination that bees perform is a vital task for the survival of agriculture. Virtually all fruits and many vegetables rely on bees for pollination, and it is estimated that bees are responsible for pollinating 80 percent of all food crops in the United States, which amounts to around $40 billion each year.

Bees literally keep plants and crops alive, and without them, crop yields would decline dramatically. This would likely have a cumulative effect up the food chain, meaning that the animals that rely on those plants for food would also be impacted, reducing the amount of meat available for people. With the supply and demand for food drastically shifting, food prices would skyrocket. Without bees, other insects may eventually take over the empty ecological niche, but in the short and medium terms, it would mean widespread economic hardship and famine, potentially posing a threat to human survival.

So, is there currently a problem? Yes. Bees are dying at an alarming rate because of pesticides, pollution, and environmental degradation. It has been estimated that in the last year alone, up to 30 percent of the national bee population has disappeared. Experts say that this trend needs to be reversed very quickly, because if the bees die out, agriculture as we know it will collapse, so there'll be a lot more to worry about than what to put on your morning toast.

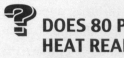

## DOES 80 PERCENT OF A PERSON'S HEAT REALLY ESCAPE FROM THEIR HEAD?

When it comes to bundling up on a cold winter's day, a warm hat is obligatory. After all, everybody knows that we lose 80 percent of our body heat through our head, or so they say. Is there any truth to this?

No. The head represents about 10 percent of the body's total surface area. If the head were to lose 80 percent of the body's heat, it would have to lose more than forty times as much heat per square inch as every other part of the body. Richard Ingebretsen of the University of Utah School of Medicine believes the real reason we lose heat through our head is because most of the time when we're outside in the cold, we're clothed. "If you don't have a hat on, you lose heat through you head, just as you would lose heat through your legs if you were wearing shorts," Ingebretsen says.

A number of studies have been conducted on the subject. In a study reported in the 2008 *BMJ* (formerly the *British Medical Journal*), participants were tested in cold water, with and without wet suits, sometimes with heads submerged and sometimes not. It was found that the head accounts for about 7 percent of the body's surface area, and the heat loss from it is fairly proportional to the amount of exposed skin. A similar study in 2013 by Thea Pretorius from the University of Manitoba found similar results—having a person's head immersed in cold water only added 10 percent to the person's overall heat loss.

So, where did this myth begin? Experiments conducted in the 1950s by the US military found that most of a person's heat was in fact lost through the head. However, the volunteers were dressed in Arctic survival suits in bitterly cold conditions, and their only exposed area was their head. Probably based on this, the *US Army Field Manual* from the 1970s claimed that 40 to 45 percent of a person's body heat is lost through the head. In situations such as this, where the body is covered and the head is exposed, a greater percentage of heat will escape from the head and the body's core temperature will drop at a disproportionate rate. But when both the body and the head are completely covered or completely uncovered, the heat loss from the head will generally be proportional to the surface area of the head; that is, around 10 percent.

## HOW IS THE NAME OF THE PAINTER VAN GOGH PRONOUNCED?

Dutch post-impressionist painter Vincent Willem van Gogh is among the most famous and influential figures in the history of art. He was a prolific artist, painting 2,100 works in just over a decade. Characterized by bold colors and dramatic brushwork, his works today fetch astronomical prices, in the tens of millions of dollars. He was 37 when he died in 1890, and at that time, having virtually never sold a painting, he would have been shocked to think of the conjecture that now surrounds the pronunciation of his name. So, is it van "Go" or van "Goff"?

Technically, neither.

In the United States, the name is usually pronounced as van "Go," while in Britain they tend to say van "Goff." However, neither of these is considered correct in van Gogh's homeland of the Netherlands. The Gogh is actually pronounced "Hockh," with the "-kh" having a glottal sound like the Scottish *loch*. Put more simply, the correct pronunciation is essentially "Hok."

The reasons for the common mispronunciation are twofold. The glottal sound of the -gh does not exist in the language of the United States or Britain (except in Scotland and Wales). In addition, the name van Gogh emerged well before the spread of spoken mass media. Any references to the painter's name would have been read, rather than heard, meaning that alternative pronunciations were very likely to occur.

However, despite the fact that the technically correct way to say Gogh in Dutch is Hok, for whatever reason, Vincent didn't say it that way. Perhaps he thought it was too difficult for people to say, or his family didn't actually use that pronunciation. The artist was habitually annoyed by people saying van Go, so whenever he had to sign a register book, he would write his name phonetically as van Goff in the hope that people would say it that way. This provides a cogent argument that van Goff is how the name should be pronounced.

Given that nobody will know who you're talking about if you say van Hok anyway, and the fact that Vincent himself pronounced it van Goff, van Goff is the logical choice.

#  WHAT EXACTLY IS INTERPOL?

You hear it in espionage movies all the time. The bad guy flees, usually to somewhere in Europe, and the next minute the director of the FBI is advising Interpol and asking for assistance. But does anyone know what Interpol actually is?

The full name of Interpol is the International Criminal Police Organization, or the ICPO. It was established as the International Criminal Police Commission in 1923 and chose Interpol as its telegraphic address in 1946, making that its common name in 1956. The United Kingdom joined Interpol in 1928, and the United States joined in 1938.

Interpol is an international police agency that helps other law enforcement agencies track criminals who operate across national borders. It is a network of police forces from 190 countries, and every member country has its own Interpol office, which connects that country's police force with the other members. They share information with each other, and the organization's databases, communications protocols, and international notices are vital tools in the fight against international crime.

Interpol helps police forces keep informed of international crimes via notices. Notices are a type of alert message that are sent to all member countries. They can be requests for information, warnings, or, just like in the movies, wanted notices. Interpol is also the owner of I-24/7, a highly secure network that members can use to search Interpol's international criminal databases. When they say in the movies to "run the fingerprints against all known databases," it will likely be done via the powerful I-24/7.

The Command and Coordination Center (CCC) is the central hub for Interpol's work. It has branches in Lyon, France, and Buenos Aires, Argentina. The CCC is manned 24 hours a day throughout the year by staff from all over the world. Interpol's annual budget is around 78 million Euro, most of which is provided through member contributions.

The upshot of all this is, do whatever you can to avoid getting on Interpol's radar. It is a very serious and powerful organization.

## WHY DO SUPERHEROES WEAR THEIR UNDERWEAR ON THE OUTSIDE?

Over the years, many superheroes have been known for one particular costume characteristic—wearing a pair of color-contrasting underwear on top of their pants. It became normal to see Superman's red underwear over his blue pants, or Batman's black underwear over his gray uniform. Is this bizarre phenomenon merely a fashion faux pas that persisted, did they lack fashion role models because they lost their parents at an early age, or was it to distract people from focusing on how much they actually looked like their daytime persona? Just how did this superhero clothing convention begin?

It wasn't a mistake. Early superheroes were modeled on the circus performers and wrestlers of the time, who often wore trunks over a set of tights. Since superheroes are generally associated with feats of athleticism and strength, it was logical to emulate the garb of these real-life athletes. Two of the earliest examples of this were Flash Gordon in 1934 and Superman in 1938. Julius Schwartz, the editor of *DC Comics* (which included Superman) from 1944 to 1986, confirmed this as the origin of the practice.

But at the risk of pedantry, it should be noted that these early wrestlers, circus performers, and superheroes weren't actually wearing underwear. The outer layer was tight underwear-like shorts over their leggings. And that makes it all OK.

## DOES WATCHING VIOLENT TELEVISION INFLUENCE CHILDREN?

A 1999 report by the Senate Judiciary Committee estimated that the average American child will see 200,000 violent acts and 16,000 murders on television by age 18. Two-thirds of all programming contains violence, and virtually since the dawn of television, parents, teachers, and mental health authorities have been warning against the impact of violent television on children. Is there a genuine basis for this concern?

Behavioral psychologists will confirm that children learn from experience and role modeling. Because of this, when they see violence on television, they sometimes have a tendency to emulate it, thinking that it is an acceptable way to behave. Viewing violence is also thought to affect a child's empathy, as well as make the child more likely to use aggressive strategies to solve problems. To address these concerns, the Surgeon General's Scientific Advisory Committee on Television and Social Behavior was formed in 1969 to assess the impact of television violence on people. The resulting report, as well as a follow-up report in 1982 by the National Institute of Mental Health, identified a number of major effects of viewing violence: Children may become less sensitive to the pain and suffering of others; children may be more fearful of the world around them; and children may be more likely to behave in an aggressive or harmful way.

Literally thousands of studies since the 1950s have shown a clear link between the exposure to violence on television and violent behavior.  In 1977, psychologists L. Rowell Huesmann and Leonard Eron from the University of Michigan researched the issue with a longitudinal study of 557 children. They found that elementary school children who watched a lot of television violence tended to exhibit much higher levels of aggressive behavior as teenagers. In 2003, 329 of the original children, then in their twenties, were surveyed again. The results strongly linked watching violence as children with committing violence. The adults who were high viewers of television violence as children were much more likely to have assaulted their spouses and were three times as likely to have been convicted of a crime. The findings held true for any child from any family, regardless of the child's sex, initial aggression levels, social status, or the parenting style they had received.

So, does watching violent television influence children? Yes. An overwhelming amount of evidence says that it does.

## ❓ CAN POLICE DOGS REALLY SNIFF OUT DRUGS?

The German shepherd, Belgian Malinois, and Labrador retriever breeds possess an incredible sense of smell, as well as strong hunting instincts. Coupled with their extensive training, these attributes make them excellent police sniffer dogs, highly driven to detect and seek out illicit substances. But just how good are they? What's their success rate?

Sniffer dogs undergo intensive training. It usually involves a white towel. Dogs love to play a game of tug-of-war with a towel, so the handler plays it with the dog, later rolling a bag of drugs up inside the towel. After playing for a while, the dog starts to associate the smell of the drugs with the smell of its favorite toy. The handler then hides the towel, with the drugs inside. When the dog sniffs it out, it is rewarded with a game of tug-of-war. It soon comes to learn that finding the towel (and drugs) earns a reward. Different drugs are later placed in the towel until the dog is able to sniff out a number of illegal substances.

But, despite this training, some people remain skeptical. In 2011, the *Chicago Tribune* claimed that the dogs' responses are influenced by the biases and behaviors of their handlers. After examining three years of data for dogs used in roadside traffic stops, it was claimed that only 44 percent of the dogs' positive signals led to the  discovery of drugs. The analysis also showed that stops of Hispanic drivers only yielded a 27 percent success rate.

Another study, published by Lisa Lit in the journal *Animal Cognition* in 2011, also brings into question the effectiveness of sniffer dogs. Researchers placed packages inside a church and led the handlers to believe that certain packages contained drugs, when in fact, none of them did. Despite there never being any drugs whatsoever placed in the church, 225 alerts were issued by the 18 handlers and their dogs, all of them incorrect. Indeed, drastically more false alarms occurred in places were red markers were positioned to indicate the presence of drugs to the handlers.

Dog behavioral experts believe these skewed statistics are the result of dogs relying on cues from their handlers, whether the cues are intentional or subconscious. Dogs have been shown to rely more heavily on human cues, such as eye contact, glances, and body orientation, than their own sight and smell when looking for food. A classic example is how a dog generally prefers to look for food in an empty bowl that a human is pointing to rather than a full bowl of food that it can see and smell.

With these studies in mind, can sniffer dogs really be trusted to detect drugs? Perhaps, but it seems the subjective opinion of the police dog handler might be just as influential as the dog's heightened sense of smell.

## WHY DIDN'T NATIVE AMERICANS WIPE OUT EUROPEANS WITH DISEASES?

Up to 50 million people lived in the Americas when the European colonists arrived, and around 95 percent of them were killed by European diseases, far more than through war or acts of violence. But why didn't it work the other way? Why weren't 19 out of 20 Europeans killed by Native American diseases?

Europeans had more robust immune systems for the following reasons:

1. **Animals.** Europeans had been surrounded by domestic animals for thousands of years and had grown immune to many diseases as a result. A significant percentage of human diseases comes from domestic animals, and the more that people are exposed to them, the more tolerant they become. Native Americans, on the other hand, were largely hunters and gatherers, and the llama was the only livestock domesticated in the Americas. Even still,

llamas are not milked, do not live in large herds, and don't live in barns and huts alongside humans. This lack of close contact would have prevented the significant exchange of germs between llamas and people.

2. **Population.** Diseases need large and dense populations to sustain themselves. European cities had high population densities and poor sanitation, allowing diseases to spread quickly and easily take hold. This exposed the Europeans to numerous pathogens, and their immune systems adapted to the diseases and thrived. Native American populations, on the other hand, were low density and isolated from each other. This meant that a disease would kill out an entire village and end there because of a lack of additional hosts. This prevented the native people from building up strong immune systems.

3. **Travel and exchange.** Groups of people and animals moved around a lot in Europe because of war and trade, spreading their diseases across countries as they did. Europeans interacted with Asia, the Middle East, and North Africa. Extensive travel provides an ideal mechanism for spreading and maintaining epidemics. This increased the immune systems of any disease survivors, who were exposed to far more types of pathogens than Native Americans, who did not come into contact with foreign peoples.

These three factors meant that the Native Americans didn't have many diseases to pass onto the Europeans, who were able to ward off most of what did exist. On the other hand, the many and varied diseases brought by the Europeans were new to the Native Americans, killing millions of them.

It wasn't all one-way traffic, though. Chagas disease, a tropical parasitic disease, originated in the New World, and many scientists believe another highly infectious disease was brought from the Americas back to Europe by the crew of Christopher Columbus—syphilis.

## WHAT HAPPENS TO STUFF CONFISCATED AT SECURITY CHECKPOINTS?

As anyone from the Transportation Security Administration will tell you, the TSA does not confiscate banned goods; the passenger surrenders them. Passengers can return to the airline's ticketing counter and check the goods in, or give them to someone not traveling. Or, they can surrender them. Many people assume that the TSA employees take their pick of the bounty for their own personal use, but that is not the case, and it is illegal to do so. So, what happens to the "voluntary abandoned property" that the TSA confiscates?

1. **Evidence.** Any illegal items, such as drugs or guns, are handed over to local authorities as evidence for investigation, with the person who had them often facing prosecution.

2. **Disposal.** The bottles of liquids and gels that fill the huge trash bins that you see at the security gates are destroyed for quarantine reasons. The TSA doesn't have the manpower to test them all, so it's easier to just dispose of them in bulk.

3. **Donations.** Many useful items are donated to local non-profit organizations, such as schools, charities, and police departments. Those items are then put to use or sold by the particular organization.

4. **Reselling.** Under federal law, the TSA is not allowed to profit from any item that it confiscates. However, state agencies can. The TSA hands a lot of items over to the state, who then sells them at surplus centers or online auction sites, such as eBay. And what are the most commonly sold items? Knives, baseball bats, and numerous pairs of scissors. And for good money too. According to an official report, the state of Pennsylvania made around $800,000 in revenue from selling confiscated property online between 2004 and 2012.

# ? WHAT IS THE DIFFERENCE BETWEEN A SEAL AND A SEA LION?

There's a good reason why seals and sea lions look so similar. They're both part of the pinniped taxonomic group, a name that means "fin footed." Walruses are also part of the group, but are easily recognizable by their prominent tusks. Seals and sea lions are more difficult to distinguish, but have a number of differences.

*Seal (top) and sea lion (bottom)*

1. **Ears.** At a glance, the most obvious difference between the two animals is the ears. While sea lions have small ear flaps, seals only have tiny holes on the sides of their heads, with no external ears.

2. **Groups.** Seals are typically loners and lead solitary lives, coming ashore together only once a year to mate. They are also quiet animals, vocalizing via soft grunts. Sea lions, on the other hand, congregate in large gregarious herds of up to 1,500 individuals. Sea lions are also much larger, as well as louder, often barking noisily at each other.

3. **Habitat.** While both species spend time in and out of the water, seals are better adapted to the water. They are sleeker than sea lions and far more aquadynamic. They also have hind flippers that angle backward and don't rotate, and stubby front feet. This makes them

fast in the water but cumbersome on land. Sea lions, however, have elongated fore flippers and hind flippers that can rotate forward. This allows them to "walk" on land by levering their hind flippers underneath their larger bodies.

So, while they may look similar at first blush, seals and sea lions are actually very different animals.

## ❓ WHY DO BUGS ROLL ONTO THEIR BACKS WHEN THEY DIE?

If you've ever tried to kill a large bug with insect spray, you know that you haven't really won the battle until the bug is lying on its back with its legs sticking up in the air. Why do dead or dying bugs assume this familiar death pose?

Many bugs have an exoskeleton, which is a strong, shell-like covering. While the shell protects them against predators and the elements, it is heavy. Normally, if a healthy bug is

knocked onto its back, it can use its legs to rock onto its side and right itself. However, when a bug ingests an insecticide, the bug's neuro-transmitters are disrupted and its nervous system shuts down. This severely hampers the bug's coordination, and it goes into convulsions and loses the ability to synchronize all of its legs. This causes its legs to collapse and the bug to topple over onto its shell. The bug is then too weak to be able to right itself, and it remains stuck on its back. While on its back, the bug is unable to obtain nutrients or protect itself from predators, and if it doesn't have the strength to flip back over, it soon dies.

In addition to insecticides, a bug may collapse through aging, an injury, or malnourishment. These factors will also reduce a bug's strength, often causing it to topple onto its back and die, legs in the air.

## WHAT DOES THE ZIP IN "ZIP CODE" MEAN?

ZIP codes are a system of postal codes that were put in place by the United States Postal Service in 1963. The idea was to allow the postal service to more efficiently route mail. But what does the ZIP stand for, and how did it come about?

ZIP stands for zone improvement plan. The basic format consists of five numerical digits, but it was twenty years in the making.

In 1943, two-digit postal zone numbers were introduced for many large cities. The number represented a specific zone within a city. Then, in 1944, Robert Moon, an employee of the post office, submitted a proposal for an additional three digits to signify the sectional center facility, or SCF, within the city. The SCF sorts the mail to all post offices with those first three digits in their ZIP codes. The mail is then sorted according to the final two digits, which represent the specific zone, and is sent to the corresponding post offices. In the case of large cities, those last two digits are the same as the old postal zone numbers.

In 1963, these five-digit ZIP codes were introduced nationwide. An extended ZIP+4 code was introduced in

1983. It included the five-digit ZIP code, plus four additional digits to determine a more specific location within the ZIP code, such as a group of apartments, to aid in efficient mail sorting and delivery. The plus-four code, however, was met with public resistance and is not mandatory.

Today, the ZIP code, which is often translated into an Intelligent Mail barcode that is printed on a mail item to facilitate automated sorting, is set out as follows: The first digit represents the state, the next two digits the SCF, and the fourth and fifth digits the area of the city, or the particular town.

 ## WHY DO YOU SOMETIMES SEE A PAIR OF SNEAKERS HANGING OVER POWER LINES?

In almost any city you visit around the world, at some point you'll see somebody's shoes, laces tied together, hanging over a power line. Known as shoe tossing, it usually involves sneakers and is most prevalent in urban areas or college neighborhoods. Despite its widespread nature, it has evoked much curiosity over the years, and there is no universal explanation for the practice. Here are a number of theories.

1. **Drugs.** One of the prevailing theories is that the sneakers are used to pinpoint a drug-dealing zone. They act as a sign to alert prospective purchasers that drugs are available nearby, so if a person loiters near the hanging shoes, a drug dealer may approach.

2. **Gang turf.** The hanging sneakers may also indicate that a certain gang is claiming the territory. This is

related to the drug theory; if the area is home to a gang, drugs are also likely to be available.

3. **Celebration.** The sneakers can indicate an act of celebration, marking a rite of passage, like a graduation from school or college. They have even been known to mark someone losing their virginity, or to mark an upcoming marriage. The custom may have originated with members of the military, who are said to have thrown their boots over power lines when they completed their basic training.

4. **Commemoration.** People sometimes throw the shoes to commemorate the life of someone who has died.

Legend has it that when the person's spirit returns, it will be able to walk above the ground, closer to Heaven. They are also sometimes thrown to signal that someone is leaving the neighborhood and moving on to better things.

5. **Bullying.** Many people believe that it is simply a form of bullying, the bully stealing someone's shoes and throwing them to an irretrievable place. Others say it's done as a practical joke played on drunkards.

6. **Protest.** The sneakers may be thrown as a mark of protest against the government or other authority if the neighborhood is unhappy with a law or decision.

7. **Art.** Yet another theory is that the thrown sneakers represent art, or a manifestation of the human instinct to leave their mark on their surroundings.

It's likely that one or more of the above theories are correct, and the precise meaning of the hanging sneakers varies with the individual location. Like many human practices, it seems to have taken on new meanings as it's spread. But one thing is for sure, the urge in people to launch their sneakers at power lines, hoping they'll hang there forever, seems to be universal.

 **DOES SUGAR MAKE KIDS HYPER?**

Many parents will attest to the fact that a single bite of birthday cake will turn their polite and perfectly behaved angel into a maniacal demon who runs around the room terrorizing everyone and everything. Anyone who's been to a toddler's birthday party will probably agree that this hypothesis sounds reasonable, but does a small, sugary treat really lead to a hyperactive frenzy?

The research says no. Not at all.

Dr. Mark Wolraich, the chief of Developmental and Behavioral Pediatrics at the Oklahoma University Health Sciences Center, studied the effects of sugar on children in the 1990s. His 1994 study published in *The New England Journal of Medicine* found that sugar does not appear to affect behavior in children. Instead, he found that it was the parents' expectations of so-called sugar highs that colored the way they viewed their children's behavior. He said that children tended to be more hyperactive at birthday parties because they were excited, not because of the sugar they had eaten. Parents, however, make the incorrect link.

Indeed, a 1994 study reported in the *Journal of Abnormal Child Psychology* found parents to be more likely to say their child was hyperactive even when the "sugar" fix was a placebo. Half the mothers in the study were told their children had been given a sugary drink, and it was these mothers who rated their children as more hyperactive. These mothers were also more likely to criticize their children, thinking they were behaving badly because of the "sugar."

In another 1994 study published in the *New England Journal of Medicine*, three sets of children were given three different diets for three weeks. One diet was high in sugar, one high in a noncaloric sweetener, and one with no sweetener. Neither the families nor the researchers knew which children were on which diet. According to the cognitive and behavioral tests, as well as reports from the researchers, parents, and teachers, there were no significant differences among the children on the three diets, indicating that sugar did not affect their intellect or behavior in any way.

In 1995, Dr. Mark Wolraich also conducted a review of sixteen studies done on the topic. The statistician who looked at the results said that "he had never had such consistently negative results," meaning that sugar did not correlate to hyperactivity.

So, how did the sugar high myth arise? The misconception comes from the idea that increased blood sugar levels translate into hyperactivity. It is true that someone with low blood-sugar levels can get an energy boost from sugar, but the body will normally regulate those sugars. If the body needs energy, it will use it, and if it doesn't, the sugar will be converted into fat for storage. In fact, sugar can have a soothing effect, temporarily increasing calming neurochemicals in the brain, such as serotonin.

So, should you give your child sugary drinks and food? While there are plenty of good reasons not to feed your children excess sugar, such as potential weight gain and dental deterioration, the fear of them turning into crazed sugar monsters who run around the house destroying everything in their path is not one of them.

## WHERE DID THE IDEA OF COUNTING SHEEP COME FROM?

Counting sheep is a mental exercise used as a means of putting oneself to sleep. The idea is to envision an endless series of identical white sheep jumping over a fence and count them in your mind: one sheep, two sheep, three sheep, four sheep, and so on. This is done to induce boredom while occupying the mind with something simple, rhythmic, and repetitive, qualities that are known to be soporific. While it is rarely used as a solution for insomnia, it has been referenced in cartoons and mass media for so many years that it has become ingrained into popular culture's notion of sleep. But just how did this strange practice develop in the first place?

It is believed that the idea began with ancient shepherds who used communal grazing land. They were required to keep a close count of their flocks, and so religiously counted them every night before they went to sleep, the tedious practice increasing their somnolence.

Somewhat surprisingly, the concept has been recorded in literature for hundreds of years. According to *Disciplina Clericalis*, a text written in early 12th-century Spain from Islamic sources, there was a king who would be told stories each night from his storyteller. One night, the king did not want to go to sleep and demanded more stories. Himself tired, the storyteller came up with an ingenious solution and, in an attempt to put the king to sleep, told the story of a farmer who had to transport 2,000 sheep across a river, but could only put two in the boat at a time. The story required each sheep to be counted, but no more than two at a time.

The 1605 Spanish book by Miguel de Cervantes, *Don Quixote*, reworked this earlier story, but substituted goats for sheep. Then, in 1832, Harriet Martineau's *Illustrations of*

*Political Economy* referenced counting sheep as a means of falling asleep: "It was a sight of monotony to behold one sheep after another follow the adventurous one…the recollection of the scene of transit served to send the landowner to sleep more than once."

Despite the ancient origins of the practice, it has been shown to be ineffective as a sleeping aid. A 2002 Oxford University study found that insomniacs who counted imaginary sheep actually took longer to fall asleep. Perhaps that's why Don Quixote preferred goats.

## ❓ DID EINSTEIN REALLY FAIL MATH AS A CHILD?

Albert Einstein was a German-born theoretical physicist who developed the ground-breaking theory of relativity, which explains how space, time, and gravity interact, and is widely thought to be one of the pillars of modern physics. He is arguably the most famous and brilliant scientist in history, but there are commonly held beliefs about his childhood that conflict with the genius that he was. One particular myth states that he was a bad student who flunked math. Is there any truth to this outlandish claim? How could he have completed the work he did without being good at math?

In 1935, a rabbi at Princeton showed Einstein a clipping of a newspaper column with the headline "Greatest living mathematician failed in mathematics." Einstein just laughed at that suggestion and went on to explain that he never failed math, and that in primary school he was at the top of his class. By age eleven, he was reading college physics textbooks, and his sister said that by age twelve he was solving complicated problems in applied arithmetic, and began learning geometry and algebra on his own. His parents bought him the textbooks for these disciplines well in advance of the school curriculum. Not only did he learn the proofs in the books, he tackled the new theories by trying to solve them on his own, coming up with a unique way of proving the Pythagorean theorem. Einstein said that before he was fifteen, he had mastered differential and integral calculus. Clearly a gifted child, his favorite book at age thirteen was Kant's *Critique of Pure Reason*.

The answer to the question is that, no, Einstein did not fail math as a child, and was in fact exceptional at the subject. So, where did this idea come from?

It probably originated from the fact that at age sixteen he failed the entrance exam to the Zurich Polytechnic. However, he was nearly two years from graduating high school at the time and had not learned much French, the language in which the exam was given. Nevertheless, he did well in the math section but failed the language, botany, and zoology sections.

Einstein did hate his early years at school, particularly the strict protocols and rote learning demanded of students. And he skipped classes and angered professors because he preferred to study on his own. Despite all of that, he was an exceptional math student and gained high marks from an early age.

If anyone did doubt his math ability, in 1921 he received the Nobel Prize in Physics "for his services to theoretical physics, and especially for his discovery of the law of the photoelectric effect," which was a pivotal step in the evolution of quantum theory. If any of that makes any sense to you, you will know that it requires some pretty advanced math equations.

## ? ARE ZEBRAS' STRIPES BLACK OR WHITE?

What's black and white and eats like a horse? A zebra. Zebras are distinctive on the plains of Africa because of their black and white striped coats. Typically vertical on the head, neck, front quarters, and main body, and horizontal at the rear and on the legs, the patterns of striping are unique to each individual animal and serve a number of purposes.

The stripes may help cool the zebra by promoting air flow across the animal (the air may move more quickly over the black, light-absorbing stripes and more slowly over the white stripes), but camouflage is the most commonly held explanation for the stripes. The vertical striping may help hide the zebra in grass by disrupting its outline. The stripes may also serve to confuse predators by what's called motion dazzle. A

group of zebras together may appear as one large mass of flickering stripes, making it difficult for a predator to isolate a specific target.

Whatever the reason for the stripes, the age-old question still persists—are they black or white?

It was traditionally believed that zebras were white animals with black stripes, since many zebras have white underbellies. However, the striped pattern of zebras comes about from a genetic process called selective pigmentation. This means that black is the predominant and actual color of the zebra's coat, and the part that contains very little pigmentation appears as white. As a zebra embryo develops, it starts out completely black. The white stripes then emerge as the genes that code for the dark pigment melanin, which makes the hair black, are selectively deactivated for the hair follicles that cover certain areas of the skin. This results in the white stripes.

Corroborating the fact that the stripes of zebras are white, if you shaved a zebra, a completely black-skinned animal would remain.

## WHY CAN'T MEN SEE THINGS THAT ARE RIGHT IN FRONT OF THEM?

Him: "Where's the butter?" Her: "In the fridge." Him: "I can't see it. It's not there." Her: "It's in the middle of the top shelf." Him: "Nope, can't see it." She then walks over and, as if by magic, grabs the butter immediately. Sound familiar? Men think this is a trick and accuse women of hiding things.

Women think men deliberately play dumb purely to annoy them. Why is it that men can't seem to see things that are right in front of them?

The vision of men and women differs significantly. Women have a greater variety of cone-shaped cells in their eyes, which gives them superior color vision, as well as wider peripheral vision. Why? Evolution.

As the women of our ancestors were nest defenders, their eyes developed to give them a broad spectrum of vision. They can see an arc of at least 45 degrees to each side of the head, as well as the same arc above and below the nose. Women evolved this way to facilitate multitasking. They were required to cook and look after the dwelling, be it a cave or otherwise, and also tend to the children and ensure their safety. They had to be alert to danger from any angle while they undertook these various tasks at the same time. Their eyes evolved this way to help them.

Men, on the other hand, were hunters, and evolved with a long-distance type of tunnel vision. This allowed them to see accurately over great distances, like a pair of binoculars. This was essential in spotting distant prey and singularly focusing on that prey while in pursuit. Peripheral vision was not as important for men, so, even now, their eyes have difficulty seeing single small objects that are nearby, especially when those objects are intermingled with other items, like the butter in the fridge.

So, ladies, don't despair. You can rest assured that the men in your life are not simply trying to annoy you. It's a biological fact that they sometimes genuinely can't see things that are right in front of them.

# ❓ WHY ARE THE ACADEMY AWARDS CALLED THE OSCARS?

Every year the Academy Awards in Hollywood showcases the most talented and glamorous stars of the film industry. Since the inception of the Academy Awards in 1929, the winners of each category have been awarded a copy of a golden statuette, officially called the Academy Award of Merit, but more commonly known by its nickname, Oscar. How did this seemingly unrelated moniker come about?

The origin of the name Oscar is disputed.

Some believe that Bette Davis, a president of the Academy, named the trophy after her first husband, the band leader Harmon Oscar Nelson. However, the most popular theory is that the nickname was coined by the Academy librarian and future Director of the Academy of Motion Picture Arts and Sciences, Margaret Herrick. It is said that when Herrick first saw the statue in 1931, she said that it looked like her Uncle Oscar, a nickname she used for her cousin Oscar Pierce. Apparently, the columnist Sidney Skolsky was there at the time, and in a 1934 *New York Daily News* article, mockingly referred to the statue as the Oscar.

Others claim that Skolsky merely took the idea from Walt Disney's Academy Award acceptance speech for *Three Little Pigs* in 1934, the same year that Skolsky first covered the Awards. Disney referred to the statue as the Oscar, which was supposedly an already well-established nickname for it within the industry. Skolsky continued to use the name over the ensuing years until it became the accepted name.

In the end, nobody really knows for sure how the nickname came about, but the Academy officially adopted the name Oscar for the statue in 1939, and in 2013, the Academy Awards themselves were officially rebranded as The Oscars.

## WHAT ARE THE ORIGINS OF THE EXPRESSION "KNOCK ON WOOD"?

"Knock on wood" is often heard to express a wish that something will or will not occur. It's almost used in a joking attempt to prevent someone from being jinxed, such as, "I've not yet lost on the stock market, knock on wood." The person will sometimes physically tap a piece of wood, like a table top, when making such a comment. What are the origins of this bizarre phrase?

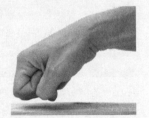

Sometimes phrased as "touch wood," knock on wood is an expression that dates back to the ancient Druids, a race that inhabited England before the Romans. The Druids worshipped trees (in particular, oaks) and held the firm belief that protective spirits lived within trees. Trees, they believed, were sources of good and warded off evil spirits. People in need of good luck would go and touch a tree. Others actually wore small pieces of oak on necklaces so the wood was always in contact with their skin to bring them good luck.

The expression became commonplace by the 1850s, and Winston Churchill once said that he always liked to be within an arm's length of a piece of wood.

# ❓ WHAT HAPPENS IF A PERSON IS TRANSFUSED WITH THE WRONG BLOOD TYPE?

Everyone has one of four blood types they inherit from their parents: A, B, AB, or O. Type O is the most common, followed by A, then B, with AB the least common. All blood looks the same and we're all human, so why are the blood banks always saying they're short of a certain type of blood? What's the difference? Why can't any type of blood be used for any person?

While all blood is similar in its components—red cells, platelets, and plasma—it also has another important characteristic that makes it unique: antigens.

Type A blood contains proteins known as A antigens. Type B blood has B antigens, type AB blood has both A and B antigens, and type O blood has no antigens. You can't receive blood that contains an antigen different from those in your blood.

This means:

- Type O blood can be universally donated, but can only be replaced by type O blood.
- Type AB blood can only be donated to people with type AB blood, but can be replaced by any type of blood.

- Type A blood can only be donated to people with type A or AB blood, and can only be received by type A or type O blood.
- Type B blood can only be donated to people with type B or AB blood, and can only be received by type B or type O blood.

Is it a big deal if you get the wrong type of blood? Yes, a very big deal.

An ABO incompatibility reaction can occur. If this happens, your immune system will attack the donor blood cells as if they are foreign invaders. It will produce antibodies against those foreign blood antigens and destroy them. This can lead to a variety of symptoms, including breathing difficulties, nausea, chest and abdominal pain, kidney failure, circulatory collapse, and death. Fortunately, an ABO reaction is a rare occurrence and only occurs as a result of severe human error, something that doctors are very careful to safeguard against.

## WHY ARE THE PORTHOLES ON SHIPS ROUND?

A porthole is generally a circular window used on the hull of a ship to admit air and light. Given that most other windows that we see are square or rectangular in shape, why are portholes different?

The forces exerted by crashing waves and heavy seas during storms are far greater than wind forces. This is the reason portholes are round. Sharp angles and corners in normal windows are a weak point and are the place where cracks usually develop. A square frame also places more stress on the middle of each of the flat sides, which can cause the window to break prematurely.

Round windows, on the other hand, have no weak points. A round window carries any stresses around the perimeter of the window and allows them to propagate back through the surface of the window, minimizing  any concentration of stress. Any force that is exerted on the window gets distributed evenly around the frame. This provides a circular window with far more structural integrity than a rectangular or square one.

Round holes are also easier to properly seal, which is important in wet conditions.

For these reasons, portholes are well-suited in circumstances where extreme pressure is likely, and they are often found in submarines and space stations.

## WHY IS A MILE 5,280 FEET LONG?

The mile is a unit of measurement that many people use every day. We refer to something as being a couple of miles up the road, the odometers in our cars measure in miles, and the distances to towns are referred to in miles on highway signs. But for such a ubiquitous measurement for distance, it contains a very strange number of feet: 5,280. How did that number come about?

The basic concept of the mile originated in Roman times. The Romans used a unit of distance called the *mille passum*, which translated to "a thousand paces," and was measured as the total distance when the left foot hit the ground a thousand times. The measure of one Roman foot was established in 29 BC, and one pace was considered to be five Roman feet. This made the Roman mile 5,000 feet. So, how did it become 5,280 feet?

As Britain was part of the Roman Empire from the 1st to 5th centuries AD, the British measuring system was influenced by the Romans. They used the Roman mile as a model but combined it with the furlong.

Now used exclusively in horseracing parlance, the furlong originated with the early British farmers. They laid out their fields in plowed furrows that were consistently 660 feet long, which was the length a team of oxen could plow in a day—one furrow long. Over time, by slurring the words, the "furrow long" became the furlong. The Roman mile was about seven-and-a-half furlongs, so to make things neater, the British lengthened it to eight furlongs, which equals 5,280 feet.

The British *Weights and Measures Act* of 1593 legally set the mile as a length containing eight furlongs, and this 5,280-foot distance was later adopted in America.

## WHY DO WEATHERVANES HAVE ROOSTERS ON TOP OF THEM?

A weathervane, also known as a weathercock, is an instrument for showing the direction of the wind. While traditionally functional, today they are generally decorative and typically placed on the highest point of a structure, such as a house. They often feature a rooster with letters indicating the points of the compass. What is the relevance of the rooster?

The answer to that question dates back nearly three thousand years.

In ancient times, people tied strings or cloths to the tops of buildings so that they could see which way the wind was blowing. Banners were later attached for this purpose, which

is where the *vane* in weathervane comes from; it's an Old English word meaning banner or flag. How did the banner transform into a rooster?

The origin is biblical and relates to the story of the Apostle Peter after the Last Supper. During the Last Supper with his disciples, Jesus predicted that Peter would deny any knowledge of him and would disown Jesus three times before the rooster crowed the next morning. Peter did deny Jesus three times, but after the third denial, he heard the rooster crow and began to cry in repentance. Because of this, the rooster became known to Christians as the symbol of St. Peter.

Sometime between 590 and 604 AD, Pope Gregory I declared that the rooster, being the emblem of St. Peter, was the most suitable symbol for Christianity, and this led to the first roosters appearing on weathervanes.

In the 9th century, Pope Nicholas decreed that all churches must display the rooster on their steeples as a reminder of Peter's betrayal of Jesus. The rooster-clad weathervane soon adorned every church and became commonplace on people's houses as well.

The oldest weathervane in existence is probably the most famous weathervane in the world. It is the Gallo di Ramperto, which is housed in Brescia, at Italy's Museo di Santa Giulia. It dates to around 820 BC and once sat on the bell tower at the Church of San Faustino in Riposo in Brescia. A rooster weathervane is also recorded in the Bayeux Tapestry, an embroidered cloth celebrating the 1066 Norman conquest of Britain. One aspect of the tapestry depicts a craftsman preparing to install a weathercock atop Westminster Abbey in London.

European settlers brought rooster weathervanes wherever they traveled, including to America, where they became an iconic symbol. Nowadays, despite being rich in history, the weathervanes are mostly ornamental, and we usually rely on the nightly meteorologists to tell us which way the wind is blowing.

## WHY DO DOGS TILT THEIR HEADS WHEN YOU TALK TO THEM?

Dogs do plenty of cute things, but few behaviors are more adorable than the head tilt, coupled with a quizzical look of confusion. Many dog owners will tell you that this endearing head tilt means that a dog is intrigued by something new, but is that the real reason? Why do dogs do it?

The following theories explain this canine predilection:

1. **Sound direction.** Even though dogs can hear frequencies that humans can't, they're actually not as good as us at determining where sounds come from. Some experts believe that when a dog tilts its head, it's adjusting its outer ears to better detect the direction of the sound. When you make an unusual sound to a dog (and it is these sorts of sounds that often elicit the head tilt), the dog might be unsure that it is coming from you and so tilts its head to make sure.

2. **Visual cues.** Dogs respond to visual and auditory cues. They have evolved to understand humans well and can read our body language, speech patterns, and facial gestures. A dog's muzzle might make it difficult to see the source of a sound and how it is being expressed because it may reduce its ability to see the lower part of your face. So by tilting its head, it is better able to see your face and read your expressions. The lower part of the  face is of particular importance, as the mouth region plays a vital role in expressing emotions. To support this, anecdotal evidence suggests that dogs with larger muzzles tend to tilt their heads more than short-muzzled dogs.

3. **Manipulation.** Some animal behavioral experts believe that the dog head tilt is little more than a Machiavellian

technique. The suggestion is that dogs recognize that we respond to the head tilt in a positive way, so they adopt that pose because they know they are more likely to receive smiles and rewards if they do. So, it could be that your dog is just using this cute trick to exploit you for attention. If so, that's one crafty canine.

 **WHY DO WE CRY AT HAPPY ENDINGS?**

How many times have you seen it—after a tumultuous emotional relationship where the outcome seems uncertain, the perfect couple is united at the end of the movie and is set to live happily ever after together? Cue the waterworks. Given that the ending is positive, what makes us respond with tears of joy?

1. **Mixed emotions.** Happy tears may be coupled with some sadness. A parent at their child's graduation, for

example, is filled with pride and happiness, but also feels a sense of loss as the child moves away from home.

2. **Safety.** Psychoanalyst Joseph Weiss proposed this view in his 1952 article "Crying at the Happy Ending." Often, we cry in films that depict loss, grief, or danger. But instead of crying while these events are occurring, we only cry when they are resolved in a satisfactory way. We may feel too imperiled to express our feelings while the situation is actually happening, because our subconscious mind is engaged in surviving or mastering that danger. The emotions we feel about the situation are repressed, only to emerge when the danger has passed and it's safe enough to express the feelings that we held at bay. Though it's just the characters in a movie going through the issues, we vicariously identify with the pain and express it as tears when it is resolved on the screen. An extreme version of this phenomenon is seen in patients with post-traumatic stress disorder. To survive extreme danger, they repress their feelings, and it is only when they return to safety that the symptoms of nightmares, panic attacks, and anxiety appear.

3. **Equilibrium.** In 2014, psychologists at Yale University proposed that people respond to a happy experience with a negative reaction in order to restore their emotional equilibrium. After running a group of volunteers through various scenarios and measuring their responses to happy reunions or cute babies, the researchers found that those who expressed negative emotions, such as crying, to positive news, were able to

moderate intense emotions more quickly and recover faster. This would have been helpful in the survival of our ancestors by allowing them to deal with an issue and, rather than dwell on it, move on quickly to overcome new adversities.

Whichever of these theories is correct, and it's likely a combination, the next time you or a friend cries at a happy ending, don't look at the resolution, but rather at the conditions that the ending resolved. They will be the underlying cause of the tears.

## WHY DO DIVERS SPIT INTO THEIR MASKS BEFORE GETTING IN THE WATER?

Thousands of divers across the world do the exact same thing before each dive—they spit into their dive mask, rub it around the lens, and then give the mask a quick rinse with sea water. Why do they engage in this perverse ritual?

Masks fog up because of a common process called condensation. When a diver is underwater, the air on the inside of the mask gets warmer due to the diver's breath and face temperature. This warm air has high energy and the water vapor molecules it contains move quickly. However, the lens of the mask cools down because of the colder water outside it. When the warmer air inside comes into contact with the cool lens, the molecules lose energy and slow down. If they slow down to a large extent, they join together and form droplets that create a fog on the inside of the mask.

The inner surface of the mask is potholed with microscopic depressions. The condensed moisture on the inside is attracted to the uneven surface and sticks to it in a fog. When spit is applied to the lens, however, it acts as a surfactant, or wetting agent, that lowers the surface tension of the droplets and creates a moisture film, allowing the droplets to spread more easily. This prevents the water vapor from forming a fog, and instead, the vapor forms bigger droplets that roll away to the edges of the mask and collect there. When the diver removes the mask, there will often be a few drops of water in it. This is fresh water, made from the humidity in their breath.

So, why is saliva used? Shampoo, detergent, soap, or alcohol also work, but spit is the most convenient surfactant—it is free, plentiful, and doesn't need to be carried around.

## WHY DO WE LIKE FOOD THAT WE HATED WHEN WE WERE YOUNGER?

Why is it that as a child you would go to extreme lengths to avoid eating broccoli, but as an adult you can't get enough of it? Is this because your palate has become more sophisticated and mature, or have you become more open-minded and adventurous? Why *do* you like foods that you hated when you were younger?

The reasons for this are both physiological and psychological.

1. **Taste buds.** Infants have around 30,000 taste buds that are spread throughout their mouths. By adulthood, only one third of these remain, mostly on our tongues. This makes eating a very intense experience for toddlers, with any flavor amplified. While maturity tends to bring an appreciation of more robust flavors, this is likely because our tasting senses have been dulled. Food that would have tasted disgusting is now more palatable. In addition, the taste buds of babies are attuned to crave fat and sugary milk. This is why a lot of young children love candy. Young children are not accustomed to salty, sour, or bitter flavors, however, which may be subconsciously rejected as potential poisons.

2. **Associations.** Because of the bitter notes in some vegetables, they are likely to taste bad to the immature (and taste bud–filled) palate. Couple this with the constant nagging from parents to eat these foods, and a negative association develops. It becomes a self-fulfilling prophecy. The more you tell yourself that you don't like something, the worse it seems.

3. **Practice.** As children get older, they often want to mimic adults, and so, will force themselves to taste certain things to feel grown up. Beer is a good example. Few people like their first bitter taste of beer, but with practice, often end up loving it. Apart from the diminution in the amount of taste buds we have, by repeatedly eating a certain food, our neuropathways develop in such a way that we genuinely start to enjoy the taste.

If you think back to the first time you tasted an oyster, it was probably repulsive. Now that you're older, it may taste exquisite. You might put this down to your sophisticated palate, but it's actually more likely a reduction in your taste buds, your developed neuropathways, and practice.

## ? WHY DO THE SPEED CONTROLS ON FANS GO FROM OFF TO HIGH TO LOW?

Have a look at the knob that controls your ceiling fan, and it will more than likely have its numerical speeds in reverse: 0 for off, 1 as the fastest setting, 2 as medium, and 3 as the slowest setting. All other electrical devices move progressively from off to the fastest, so what makes fans different?

1. **Convenience.** Most people tend to prefer the fastest setting, so that is one suggestion, though unlikely, for why it is the first one on the dial.

2. **Darkness.** Placing off next to the fastest setting allows the user to know when they've switched the fan off when it's dark and they can't see. When the fan is spinning quickly and making more noise, turning the knob one place will result in a great disparity. The person will know it's off far more easily than if it went from a slow speed to off. This, too, seems an implausible explanation.

3. **Motor function.** When the motor of a fan starts, it presents a low resistance to the electrical supply, which allows a large current to flow. This is because a fan's motor is very small. This large current flow, which can be detrimental to the fan's motor, sometimes frying it,

usually only lasts for a short period until the motor speeds up and generates enough resistance to oppose the incoming current. The faster the motor goes, the greater this resistance, or back electromotive force (back EMF). If a fan starts on a low speed, it takes longer to produce enough back EMF to limit the current, but when it starts at its fastest pace, the back EMF will rise faster and the incoming current will reduce more quickly. This protects the fan, and is the most likely reason for the order of the control settings.

## ❓ DO WE BREATHE A SINGLE MOLECULE OF JULIUS CAESAR'S LAST BREATH IN EVERY BREATH WE TAKE?

Well, that was quite a mouthful. Known as Caesar's Last Breath phenomenon, this question has become a classic teaching tool for chemistry students. Folklore has it that each time you take a breath it contains some of the molecules of Julius Caesar's last breath, the one in which he said (according to Shakespeare), "Et tu Brute? Then fall, Caesar." Is there any truth to this implausible suggestion?

As strange as it may seem, this is in fact true. It involves some very complex calculations using some very large numbers, but here it is in a nutshell. When Caesar exhaled his final breath, he released an enormous number of molecules, mostly nitrogen and carbon dioxide. By assuming the volume of his breath was one liter of air (the typical amount expelled by a person in one breath), the amount of molecules in it can be calculated to around $10^{22}$.

Assume that in the two thousand or so years since Caesar was killed, these molecules have spread throughout the entire atmosphere, mixing themselves evenly all around the world, and only a trivial amount of them has been absorbed into the oceans or the ground. Using various equations, the total amount of air in the atmosphere can be calculated as about $5.1 \times 10^{18}$ kg and would contain somewhere in the vicinity of $10^{44}$ molecules.

Further assuming that your breath is of a similar volume to Caesar's, when the molecules in the atmosphere and the molecules in a single breath are divided out, the answer is produced. If you take a deep breath right now, there's a good chance that somewhere between one and two molecules from Caesar's last breath will literally enter your lungs.

This applies to any person's last breath, but for some reason Caesar has been chosen for the conundrum. There is, however, no reason for concern, so don't hold your breath.

## WHAT CAUSES THAT RECOGNIZABLE NEW CAR SMELL?

There is nothing quite like the smell of a new car. That distinctive aroma, which many people find extremely enticing, promotes feelings of excitement and satisfaction. And despite the hundreds of varieties of cars that are available, it always smells the same. What causes it?

The new car smell comes from a combination of substances that make up the dashboard and other plastic elements inside a car. The materials used to make a car's interior include polyurethane, which is known for its durability and ability to withstand temperature changes. Polyurethane, as well as the chemicals in the adhesives and sealants that are also used, release volatile organic compounds (VOCs) into the air by a process known as outgassing. It is these compounds that create the new car smell.

Questions exist as to the danger posed by the toxicity of these VOCs. Ethylbenzene and formaldehyde, which are chemicals released from paints and glues, can cause headaches, dizziness, and allergic reactions, especially when released inside an enclosed space, such as a car's interior. In a two-year study released in 2001 by the Commonwealth Scientific and Industrial Research Organisation (CSIRO) in Australia, several health problems were found to be associated with the VOCs released in cars. Various toxic chemicals were found in new cars, including the carcinogen benzene, as well as two other possible carcinogens, cyclohexanone and styrene. These chemicals can cause disorientation, headaches, and, in large doses, cancer.

The VOCs do, however, decrease over time. In a 1995 analysis of the air from a new Lincoln Continental, the fifty VOCs that were detected had reduced by 90 percent after three weeks.

Why do we like these potentially dangerous chemicals? Scientists aren't exactly sure why the new car smell appeals to people. It may be that we associate the smell with the luxury and excitement of a new car, and so view it positively.

So much so that companies have tried to replicate it with tree-shaped air fresheners to hang off the rear view mirror.

## ❓ WHY DO ONLY CHILDREN GET HEAD LICE?

Few things are more irritating, quite literally, than a bout of head lice infecting a school. Almost all the young kids are bound to get the lice, which lead to crazed stints of scratching, day and night. But have you ever noticed that while the kids in a family seem to get head lice again and again, the parents never do? Why is it so?

Head lice are parasitic insects that live on the scalp of people, feeding off blood and causing intense itching and irritation. The lice begin as nits, which are eggs that attach to the hair shaft. After a week, a nit hatches into a baby louse called a nymph, which matures in a week. The adult louse requires human blood to live and can survive in a person's hair for up to thirty days.

There are two main reasons why children are more susceptible to head lice than adults:

1. Children tend to be in close contact with each other more regularly than adults. They are generally less protective of their personal space and have more physical contact with one another. They engage in playdates, sports activities, and slumber parties. They

also swap hats, use each other's hairbrushes, and share earphones. This makes it easy for head lice to travel from child to child.

2. The pH levels of children's scalps are also a factor. These levels are a measure of acidity. The skin of a young child has a lower level of acidity than that of an adult. When we are born, our skin pH is a neutral 7. As we grow, the body creates an acid mantle as a protective shield. This gradually increases up to the age of about twenty. This acid mantle acts as the first barrier of defense against infections and parasites. As it's not fully developed in children, it means they are more likely to get head lice.

So, how do you stop kids from getting lice? It's a mistaken belief that lice are attracted to children who are dirty or unhygienic. The best preventative measure is for children to not share hats, clothes, or hairbrushes.

## IS IT BAD TO "CRACK" YOUR KNUCKLES?

For some it's a nervous habit, for others it brings relief. Some people crack their knuckles by pulling the tip of each finger, while others bend their fingers backward away from the hand. It is thought that around 50 percent of people crack their knuckles, with men more likely to do it than women. And if you're in that knuckle-cracking number, you've surely been told many times that it leads to arthritis. So, does it? Is cracking your knuckles really bad for you?

First, let's look at the physics behind the practice and where the sound comes from.

When you crack a knuckle, the space around the joint increases, which decreases the pressure in the joint. This decreased pressure means that the gases in the synovial fluid surrounding the joint turn into microscopic bubbles, which unite to form larger bubbles. This fluid moves to fill the extra space around the knuckle, and as it does, the bubbles pop, making the sound that you hear. After the knuckle has been cracked, it generally takes about

fifteen minutes for the gases to dissolve back into fluid, so you can crack again. But does this cracking cause arthritis?

A number of studies shed light on the topic. In a 1990 study conducted in Detroit by Dr. Jorge Castellanos and Dr. David Axelrod, the hands of three hundred people over the age of forty-five were examined. Knuckle-crackers were found to have some hand swelling and a weaker grip strength, but there was no indication of increased arthritis. In a 2010 study published in the *Journal of the American Board of Family Medicine*, which looked at the hands of 329 participants, the researchers concluded that knuckle-cracking is not associated with hand arthritis. Then, a 2016 study at the Radiological Society of North America used ultrasound to analyze knuckle-cracking in real time. The volunteers were then measured for grip strength, range of motion, and damage suffered. The researchers found that cracking didn't cause any hand problems, and, in fact, cracking actually increased the range of motion in some knuckle-crackers.

Based on the current evidence, the only thing habitual knuckle-crackers need to worry about is who they are annoying in the process. And if that doesn't worry you, simply crack on.

## WHAT ARE THE CHANCES WE ARE ALONE IN THE UNIVERSE?

One of the most vexing mysteries of the universe is whether we Earthlings are alone or not. There are potentially hundreds of billions of planets in the Milky Way alone, and hundreds of billions of galaxies in the observable universe. How likely is it that our planet is the only one that contains any form of advanced life?

Various estimates of the probability of other technologically advanced civilizations existing have been made over the years.

In 1961, University of California, Santa Cruz astronomer and astrophysicist Frank Drake devised the Drake Equation as a way to determine whether extraterrestrial intelligent life has existed. The equation can be modified by various factors, but in simplistic terms, the chances of us being the only intelligent life in our galaxy, the Milky Way, is less than 1 in 60 billion.

In 2016, Adam Frank from the University of Rochester and Woodruff Sullivan from the University of Washington formulated a new equation based on Drake's work. By accounting for new knowledge obtained by the Kepler space observatory, which was launched by NASA in 2009 to survey part of the Milky Way, their calculations were more precise. They also changed the framing of the question from "how many civilizations may exist now" to "have any ever existed." Assuming that one-fifth of all stars have habitable planets in orbit around them, they too found that the odds of us being the only advanced civilization in the Milky Way are about 1 in 60 billion. Even if only one in every million stars hosts an advanced species today, that would amount to around 300,000 such civilizations in our galaxy. Frank concluded, "It is astonishingly likely that we are not the only time and place that an advanced civilization has evolved."

And that's just for our galaxy. Based on observations from the Hubble Space Telescope that NASA launched into orbit in 1990, between 125 and 250 billion galaxies are in the observable universe. Based on the estimates of the number of stars with planets orbiting them in the observable universe, even if it is assumed that only one out of a billion of these stars has planets supporting life, there would be around 6.25 billion life-supporting planets. And that's just the observable universe. Who knows what's out there beyond that.

On the basis of these observations and the staggeringly large, almost incomprehensible figures, many scientists agree that it is wildly unlikely that we are the only advanced society that has appeared, and that other intelligent life-forms now exist or have existed before us.

But if that's the case, with numbers this large, why haven't we found them, or they found us?

The leading theory is that they're just too far away. Our radio transmission technology is not even 200 years old, so by the time we sent a transmission to a planetary system 100 light-years away, it would take another 200 or so years to receive a reply. The short lifespan of beings is another potential reason. Many civilizations might have already gone extinct, or will evolve long after we're gone. Humans have only existed for a minute amount of time, so the chances of different civilizations overlapping in the overall scheme of time is remote.

Other potential reasons include: Aliens lack the technology to contact us, aliens isolate themselves, earth is deliberately not contacted, it is difficult to move great distances throughout the universe, we are not listening properly, aliens are here undetected. Or, perhaps, the aliens are just embarrassed to be seen in their shiny silver jumpsuits.

## ❓ WHY DO PIGEONS IN CITIES HAVE DEFORMED TOES?

If you've spent any time watching pigeons in cities, you know many of them have missing or swollen toes and feet, forcing them to hobble along in an ungainly fashion. It seems that pedal deformities are ubiquitous in urban pigeons all over the world. Why?

1. **Infections.** The deformities could result from infections the birds get from standing on chemicals used on roofs and building stone, or from standing in their own excrement.

2. **Frostbite.** In very cold climates, pigeons may suffer from frostbite, which damages their toes and feet.

3. **Heredity.** They may inherit the deformities that get passed down from generation to generation, perpetuating them.

4. **Entanglement.** While the above theories all have some merit, the most likely cause of their feet issues is stringfoot. In rural areas, pigeons use twigs, straw, and hay to build nests, but in urban areas, the nests are constructed with string, cotton, human hair,  and other detritus found in cities. After spending a lot of time in their nests, their feet become entangled in these materials. This can lead to constriction in the feet, which cuts off the circulation, resulting in necrosis, infection, and ultimately, deformity.

Apart from the initial pain they experience from stringfoot, pigeons are still able to survive as long as they can get food. Mind you, for all the pigeons you see with deformed feet, there are probably many that have died from their injuries.

# ❓ WHY DO YOU HAVE TO TAKE LAPTOPS OUT OF THEIR CASES AT AIRPORT SECURITY?

The Transportation Security Administration requires that all laptops be taken out of carry-on bags at airport security and passed through scanners on their own. Apart from removing your shoes and belt, taking your laptop out of its bag would have to be the most annoying thing a traveler is required to do. Some electronic gadgets, such as tablets and e-readers, can go through the scanner in your bag, so why does your laptop have to be removed and go through in its very own bin?

There are two reasons for this: 1. To better see what's in your bag; and 2. To assess the laptop itself.

Most laptops and other large electronic devices, like gaming systems and DVD players, have a thick, dense battery. X-rays cannot usually pass through the battery, meaning that illegal items, such as a knife, could be hidden under the laptop and pass through security undetected. Removing the laptop avoids this problem.

Removing the laptop also allows the security personnel to get an unobstructed view of the machine itself. It may be possible to conceal certain items under the screen of a laptop, so by looking at it carefully and in isolation, it is easier to determine if this has happened. Laptops can also be used to conceal drugs inside them. Many Colombian airport security checkpoints not only require laptops to be removed from their cases, but they also turn the laptop on to ensure it is functioning properly and does not contain drugs.

The seriousness of electronic devices concealing dangerous items was brought to light in 1988 with the bombing of Pan Am Flight 103 over Lockerbie, Scotland. The device that destroyed the plane, and killed 270 people, was a plastic explosive hidden inside a cassette player.

Since the September 11 terrorist attacks, the removal of laptops from carry-on baggage has been standard practice at all US airports.

## WHY DO YOUR LEGS WOBBLE WHEN STANDING ON A CLIFF TOP?

Why is it harder to balance when standing on a cliff top? The surface is the same as when you're standing on safer ground, but as soon as you get close to the edge, you will start to sway, overcorrect, and your legs will wobble. What causes this to happen?

Anxiety is the reason. When you stand in high places, where you perceive some danger, the anxiety you experience compromises your movement efficiency and impairs your balance. The fear causes adrenaline to pump throughout the body and brings your focus inward, disrupting subconscious task processing.

You attempt to execute simple tasks consciously, and this makes you regress to movement behaviors characteristic of earlier stages of skill acquisition. Because of this, you don't have as much control over your limbs, and because all your weight is on your legs, you begin to wobble under the pressure. A Dutch professor of movement sciences, J. R. Pijpers, studied this concept in a series of experiments from 2002 to 2006. When tracking subjects traversing on two routes on a wall, identical except that one was 0.4 meters off the ground and the other 5 meters, he found that those on the higher wall climbed far less efficiently than those on the low wall. Those on the high wall took longer, were less fluent, were more tentative, and were far more shaky.

What explains the anxiety and fear? Evolution. Humans evolved from apes who came out of the trees and walked on the ground. Functioning at dangerous heights was never a vital trait for early man, so he lost the tolerance of heights that his ancestors who lived in trees had. We evolved to be afraid of heights as a survival mechanism, because falling from a height could result in death. This kept us firmly on the ground. As a result, if we stand in a precariously high place today, we often don't cope well and our legs may wobble as a result.

## WHY ARE THE CHINESE SUPERSTITIOUS OF THE NUMBER FOUR?

Mention the number four to any Chinese person and they're likely to turn as white as a ghost. Their superstition of the number is like the Western world's dread of thirteen, but on steroids. What is the basis for this seemingly irrational fear?

Chinese is a tonal language with a relatively small number of permitted syllables. This means that there are a large number of homophonic words. Many of the numbers are homophones of other words, and so have acquired superstitious meanings. Certain numbers are believed to be auspicious or inauspicious based on the Chinese word that the number sounds similar to. The number four is of particular significance in this regard. Pronounced *si*, it sounds very similar to the word for "death" or "disease," and because of this, is considered extremely unlucky.

Tetraphobia, which is the fear of the number four, permeates all facets of life in China (and to a lesser extent, Korea, Vietnam, and Japan). Door numbers, as well as car registration numbers, generally do not contain any fours, especially not as the last digit. Some buildings don't have a numbered fourth floor, or any floor with a four in it. As a result, a building whose highest floor number is fifty, may actually only have thirty-six physical floors. Military aircraft and ships avoid the number four, and table numbers containing four are often left out at wedding dinners and other social gatherings. Hospitals are particularly averse to the number, and you'll be hard-pressed finding four in any health facility. Giving four of something is strongly discouraged, and just mentioning the number four around a sick person is taboo. Much like Friday the 13th in Western culture, April 4 is considered an exceptionally unlucky day.

Tetraphobia has also pervaded the business world. Many product lines avoid four, with cell phone and electronic companies skipping any four series. Neighborhoods that have removed four from their street names have become more sought-after, and buildings with multiples of four levels will often achieve significantly lower returns. Four is also avoided in phone numbers, security numbers, addresses, and ID numbers, as in these instances, the number is thought to personally attach to the individual. Using the number against someone can be considered a death threat, and gangs and organized crime groups employ the number for this purpose. When Beijing lost its bid to host the 2000 Olympic Games, it was speculated that their committee then held off their bid until 2008 so as to avoid the 2004 Olympics.

If you think four is bad, it gets even worse for larger numerals containing four. In the Cantonese-speaking regions, fourteen and twenty-four are considered more unlucky. Fourteen sounds like "will certainly die," and twenty-four like "easy to die." In Mandarin-speaking regions, fourteen sounds like "wants to or is going to die," while seventy-four sounds like "will certainly die," or "will die in anger."

## WHY ARE POLICE OFFICERS KNOWN AS "COPS"?

Most people refer to police officers as cops, even the police officers themselves. What are the origins of this seemingly unrelated slang term?

Some suggest that the word cop is an acronym for "constable on patrol," but that is not the case, as the word is actually an abbreviation of copper. But it does not come from the copper badges worn by early policemen, nor from the copper buttons on their uniforms.

The word actually comes from the French word *caper*, meaning "to seize or take," which came from the Latin *capere*, meaning "to take." This evolved to the medieval English word *cap*, meaning "to arrest," and from there turned into cop.

By 1859, the word cop was being used as a reference to police officers.

# ? WILL YOU GET TETANUS BY STANDING ON A RUSTY NAIL?

Remember when you were a kid and you stood on a rusty nail, or anything rusty, and your mother would go into a blind panic that you were about to contract tetanus? The next thing you knew, you were being raced off to the doctor to get a shot. Were these fears justified, or is the rusty nail–tetanus proposition yet another old wives' tale?

Tetanus is an infection of the nervous system with the *Clostridium tetani* bacteria. Spores of this bacteria are found in soil and animal feces. The spores can remain infectious in the soil for forty years. Tetanus is contracted when the spores enter your body through a wound and become active bacteria. The bacteria spreads through the bloodstream and makes a poison called tetanus toxin, which blocks nerve signals from reaching your muscles, causing severe muscular spasms.

So, do rusty nails give you tetanus? Stepping on a rusty nail can give you tetanus, but so can a new nail. Either can potentially give you tetanus if they're dirty, because it is the dirt, and not the rust, that may contain the dangerous spores. The reason behind the rusty nail belief is that if a nail has been outside long enough to get rusty, then it's more likely to have been exposed to soils containing the bacteria, and the crevices on the rust provide a place for the soil to lodge and remain. *Clostridium tetani* can  only reproduce in an oxygen-deprived setting like a puncture wound, which standing on a rusty nail will provide.

Most cases of tetanus in the United States occur in people who have not been vaccinated against it, and in these cases, without treatment, one out of three people will die.

## ❓ WHY DOES EATING FOOD MAKE YOU HOT?

Is there anything more embarrassing than having a meal at a high-end restaurant and breaking out in a lather of sweat? Just after you start eating, the beads of moisture appear on your face, neck, and hairline, and before long, they're streaming down your face. Why does this sometimes happen?

This type of food-related perspiration is called gustatory sweating and is caused by the types of food that you eat.

1. **Spicy food.** Eating spicy food will usually make you feel hot. Capsaicin, the active ingredient in chili peppers, stimulates nerve receptors in your mouth that give the sensation of heat, but this process also tricks

your nervous system into thinking that you're hot. Your body then reacts in the same way it does to a hot summer's day. The hypothalamus region of your brain sends a signal to activate your sweat glands to cool you down.

2. **Hot food.** Food that has a physically hot temperature is also likely to make you feel hot. Hot soup, for example, will raise your body temperature, often enough to activate your sweat glands.

3. **Processed food.** White bread, fast food, chocolate, and other processed food can also increase your temperature. This is because your body has to work harder to digest these foods. Just as exercise makes you sweat, so does your overactive digestive system.

4. **Salty food.** Eating food that contains a lot of salt will often increase your body's temperature. When you consume large amounts of salt, your body will sweat to expel the excess sodium.

5. **Coffee and alcohol.** Coffee contains caffeine, which stimulates your central nervous system and activates your sweat glands. Alcohol also leads to increased body heat by widening the blood vessels in your skin.

## WHY ARE AUTOPSIES PERFORMED ON CRIMINALS WHO HAVE JUST BEEN EXECUTED?

An autopsy, also known as a post-mortem, is a medical procedure used to determine someone's cause of death. It is usually done where the cause of death is not definitively known, or if there are suspicious circumstances. Given that it's pretty obvious how an executed prisoner has been killed, why do they bother doing an autopsy?

While many states don't require autopsies to be conducted on executed criminals, in some states it is law that an autopsy be carried out in any instance where a death was not by natural causes, and that includes an execution.

Despite many states not requiring the autopsy, they are still routinely carried out after executions. The main reason is to ensure that the execution was done properly. A lethal injection, which is the way executions are now done, consists of a cocktail of drugs designed to bring about a painless death by anesthesia, paralysis, and then cardiac arrest. If the anesthesia fails, however, the prisoner experiences a torturous burning pain as the lethal dose of potassium chloride enters the bloodstream. Because of the paralysis, the condemned is unable to move or scream to indicate they are in pain. The most effective way to assess the state of the anesthesia is by measuring the concentration of anesthetic in the prisoner's blood after death. The major issue with this, however, is that the anesthetic in the blood drops quickly after death, so to be of any use, it needs to be measured within about an hour, and few states move that quickly.

In addition to determining the level of anesthetic, the medical examiner also examines the site where the needles were inserted to confirm that they were placed correctly. They also check for injuries, both internal and external, to ensure the prisoner was not assaulted in any way before the execution.

# ❓ WHY DON'T WOODPECKERS GET HEADACHES?

If you hit your head against a tree trunk all day long, you'll probably end up feeling very worse for wear, as well as acquire a serious concussion. But woodpeckers do this every day, up to twenty times a second. It's what they're named for, but it doesn't even give them a headache. What makes these little birds so special?

Woodpeckers are anatomically configured to peck wood. They have strong, dense muscles in their necks and skulls that give them strength and act like a protective helmet for the brain. Unlike in humans, the woodpecker's brain is tightly confined by the muscles in its skull. They also have a special compressible bone, called the hyoid, that wraps around their skull and acts like a seat belt for their brain. This bone prevents the bird from getting concussions.

The woodpecker has other adaptations as well. Its upper beak is longer than its lower beak, and the lower beak is made of stronger bone, which helps to absorb the impact. It also has thick inner eyelids that hold the eyes in tightly and protects them.

Woodpeckers only make straight strikes to a tree and avoid head trauma by not making any side-to-side movements that might injure them by directing the force at incompatible angles to their neck muscles.

It certainly seems that a lot of evolution has gone into these wood-obsessed birds, but it is necessary, especially for males. During courtship, they hit the wood up to 12,000 times a day.

## DO YOU NEED TO WAIT 24 HOURS BEFORE FILING A MISSING PERSON REPORT?

It's a regular occurrence in movies. Someone goes missing in circumstances that seem very suspicious, but the police tell the person's loved ones that, regrettably, there's nothing they can do and a missing person report cannot be filed until twenty-four hours have passed. Is there any truth to this popular notion?

It is a common misconception that a person must be absent for at least 24 hours before being legally classed as missing. No laws require a person to wait a specific period of time before reporting a missing person.

In fact, in cases where there is evidence of violence, an unusual absence, or when a person has serious concerns, the authorities stress the importance of beginning an investigation as soon as possible. They also strongly encourage immediately reporting a missing person when that person is a senior citizen, or mentally or physically impaired. A search will usually be conducted straightaway.

For anyone missing under the age of twenty-one, it is mandatory for the report to be taken immediately and entered into the National Crime Information Center within two hours. This is set down in law under the Crime Control

Act of 1990, which was amended by a piece of legislation known as Suzanne's Law. It was named after Suzanne Lyall, a nineteen-year-old college student at the University of Albany, who disappeared in 1998.

In most common law jurisdictions, a missing person can be declared dead *in absentia* after seven years. This time frame can be reduced in exceptional cases, such as deaths in wars or mass disasters, such as the September 11 attacks.

## ❓ WHY DO WE CRAVE GREASY FOOD WHEN WE'RE HUNGOVER?

No matter how much fun you have out partying into the wee hours, the next day you're left to face the inevitable hangover that you could sell to science. While there are many so-called hangover cures out there, all you ever seem to want is some water and a big plate of the  greasiest food you can find. Just what is it about greasy food that is so enticing while you're trying to piece together the events of the night before?

A number of factors draw us to the fatty next-day fry-up.

1. **Primal instincts.** We have a biological instinct to eat the most energy-dense food available, and fatty, greasy foods provide this energy. Calorically dense food was sought by our ancestors because it takes a minimum of preparation and yields the biggest payoff. In modern times, we are usually able to control these desires,

but when suffering the effects of a hangover, our self-control is diminished and we often give in to these deeply rooted primitive instincts.

2. **Gastritis.** Excessive alcohol can cause gastritis, an inflammation of the stomach lining resulting in nausea and vomiting. Fatty foods line the stomach, reducing that acidic effect and making you feel better.

3. **Dehydration.** Alcohol is a diuretic, meaning you lose a lot more fluid than you drink. This leads to dehydration and headaches, as the necessary electrolytes in your body have been depleted. Eating salty foods, which greasy foods usually are, helps to replenish these electrolytes.

4. **Brain chemicals.** Alcohol boosts the production of the brain protein galanin, which makes us crave fat. Galanin is stimulated by triglycerides, the main constituents in human body fat and vegetable fat. These triglycerides are stored in the body's fat cells and are released by consuming both high-fat foods and alcohol. This then increases the production of galanin, which further increases our appetite for fat. This creates a fat-craving cycle. A 2004 study at Princeton University found that rats that were injected with galanin were inclined to consume more alcohol and crave more fat.

5. **Psychology.** Perhaps because it has worked for them in the past, people tend to associate a big greasy next-day breakfast with feeling better, and so resort to it time and time again. When it tastes that good and helps to take away the pain, why wouldn't you?

# ❓ DO YOU REALLY HAVE TO WAIT 30 MINUTES TO SWIM AFTER EATING?

Many children are terrified to get into the water just after eating, because it is universally accepted that swimming with a full stomach can lead to severe muscle cramping and drowning. "Wait at least thirty minutes," parents are always saying. For kids wanting to get back in the water, this can seem like an eternity. Is it sound advice, or do parents just want a post-lunch break from supervising swimmers?

It is true that the digestive process redirects some of the blood from your muscles toward your stomach's digestive tract. This reduces the blood and oxygen levels in your limb muscles, and may reduce their efficient functioning. This could potentially cause cramping, but it's unlikely. Cramps are involuntary, spasmodic contractions of the muscles, usually caused by a combination of factors, such

as dehydration, electrolyte imbalance, and neurological fatigue. The mere fact that your digestive system is working would not usually starve the other muscles of so much blood that they would cramp.

Another suggested reason for not swimming after eating is the potential for getting a stitch. A stitch usually results in a sharp, stabbing pain under the rib cage. While it's not entirely clear what causes a stitch, it's likely related to dehydration or a redirection of blood away from the diaphragm during exercise. A stitch typically results from exercise, which includes swimming, but it is not of serious concern, and the fact that you've eaten beforehand may not increase your chances of getting a stitch.

While there is a theoretical possibility that someone could get a cramp or a stitch while swimming just after eating, it is extremely unlikely that a person would then drown as a result. A swimmer could easily exit the water if this occurred, or make their way to shallower waters and simply stand up.

Neither the American Academy of Pediatrics, the United States Consumer Product Safety Commission, nor the American Red Cross offer any guidelines or warnings related to swimming after eating. Indeed, an incident of drowning from swimming on a full stomach has never been documented, and there's no research to confirm the old wives' tale.

This is good news for kids, but less so for parents who want a rest after lunch.

#  DOES BALDNESS COME FROM THE MOTHER'S SIDE?

It is commonly heard that baldness in men is inherited from the mother's side of the family. A man just has to look at his maternal grandfather if he wants to know whether he's going to go bald or not. Is there any truth to this?

Yes, a little bit. Well, sort of.

Male-pattern baldness, also known as androgenetic alopecia, is thought to be caused by an enzyme called 5-alpha reductase, which converts testosterone into dihydro-testosterone (DHT) in genetically predisposed men. DHT acts by binding to androgen receptor sites on the cells of the hair follicles to cause specific changes. It inhibits hair growth, making healthy hair follicles produce thinner and more brittle shafts of hair, eventually dying out and causing baldness.

Experts agree that male-pattern baldness is a highly heritable condition, and the androgen receptor gene is one

of the genes involved. This gene is on the X chromosome, which is inherited from the mother (the Y chromosome comes from the father). This is why some people believe that baldness comes from the mother's side.

However, it is not the only gene involved in balding, and there are a number of genes from all chromosomes that have been implicated in androgenetic alopecia. Because various genes are involved, the exact cause of baldness cannot be determined. And while it is believed that the hereditary factor is slightly more dominant on the X chromosome from the mother, research suggests that men who have a bald father are far more likely to develop male-pattern baldness than those who don't.

In the end, whether a man goes bald or not is determined by genes from both sides of the family. He's likely to have ended up with some mix of his parents' hair genes, and not just his mother's. And that's the bald truth.

## ❓ IF YOU TOUCH A BABY BIRD, WILL ITS MOTHER REALLY REJECT IT?

If there's one thing everyone knows about baby birds, it's that you're not supposed to pick them up or so much as lay a finger on a bird's egg. If you do, the mother bird will smell the residue from your hands on her baby and reject the bird immediately before abandoning the nest. The theory is that wild birds are so sensitive to the dangers posed by humans that they will fly away if they catch even the faintest whiff of human scent on their young. Is this true?

No, not at all. Despite how timid birds may be, they do not readily abandon their young, and certainly not in response to human touch. The myth probably comes from the belief that birds can detect the faintest human smell, but this is not true. Birds actually have relatively small and simple olfactory nerves, which limits their sense of smell.

There are exceptions to this, such as the vulture, who has evolved to have a good sense of smell, but most birds cannot smell well and would be very unlikely to discern the scent of a human.

Even if a bird were able to detect your scent and make a negative association with it, it is still unlikely to reject its chicks. Like most animals, birds have an innate drive to nurture their offspring, are usually very devoted to them, and are not easily deterred from taking care of them. This is particularly so as the chicks get older, because the bird will have invested more time into the babies and will not want to see its efforts go to waste.

That said, if you do see a baby bird on the ground, as a general rule, leave it alone. It is normal for a fledgling bird to spend a few days on the ground while it's mastering its flying skills, and the bird's parents will likely be watching its progression from a distance. It is only if a bird is in a very unsafe area, such as on a road or in the vicinity of some prowling cats, that you should gently pick up the chick and put it back into its nest. And, if you do this, fear not; the bird's parents will welcome it back with open wings.

## CAN YOU GET KILLED BY POKING A METAL OBJECT INTO A POWER OUTLET?

Many people, particularly parents, sometimes wonder what would happen if a child were to stick a metal object into a power outlet. It can't be that big a deal, can it? If it were, there'd be more compulsory protection on the outlets, or they'd be located out of a child's reach. Is it actually dangerous?

You bet.

If you poke a metal object into the larger slot on the left, or the small, round hole at the bottom, nothing should happen. These are the neutral and ground slots and should not be dangerous. The smaller slot on the right, however, is the hot slot from where the current flows, and if you poke a metal object in there, you will likely receive an electrical shock.

The human body is about 70 percent water, which makes it an excellent conductor of electricity. Electricity seeks a quick path to the earth, so if you are standing on the ground and are not wearing insulated footwear, the shock may be severe. If you have wet skin and are standing in a puddle of water, you're in for a real shock.

As a minimum, you may experience a headache, muscle spasms, unconsciousness, and breathing difficulties. Some of the more serious side effects include severe burns, brain damage, respiratory failure, cardiac arrest, and death.

According to the US Consumer Product Safety Commission, approximately 4,000 people per year are taken to an emergency room seeking treatment for injuries caused by electrical outlets. Nearly 50 percent of these patients are children who have poked something into an outlet. And these are just the ones who are treated. Hundreds of people never even make it to the emergency room. Don't stick metal (or any) objects into power outlets.

# ? IS IT DANGEROUS TO WAKE A SLEEPWALKER?

Many of us have heard over the years that whatever you do, don't wake someone who is sleepwalking. Sleepwalking puts a person is such a strange state that if they are woken, the shock they experience can have serious consequences, including a heart attack or brain damage for the sleepwalker.

This is a myth. Despite the urban legend, waking a sleepwalker is harmless. It is no different from waking someone who is sleeping normally. They might get a shock, but that's about it.

This shock, however, could be dangerous for the person waking up the sleepwalker. Sleepwalking occurs during stage 3 non-rapid eye movement sleep, also known as slow wave sleep. This stage of sleep is very deep, so waking a person from it is not only difficult, but once done, can leave a person in a state of cognitive impairment for up to thirty minutes. This may result in the sleepwalker waking in a startled, confused, or agitated state. Not immediately recognizing you as someone they know may cause them to strike out at you. For your own safety, it is best not to rouse a sleepwalker, but to simply guide them back to bed in their sleep.

According to the National Sleep Foundation, sleep-walking is completely normal and is very common. As much as 15 percent of the United States population sleepwalks, and almost all children have had sleepwalking episodes, generally peaking between ages four and six.

So, where did the myth that waking a sleepwalker could kill them originate? According to Dr. Mark Mahowald, a sleep specialist at Stanford University, it comes from the ancient belief that a person's soul leaves their body during sleep. Legend had it that waking a sleepwalker would then doom that person to wander soullessly forever.

And the most common sleepwalking behavior? Urination. Men will get out of bed and pee in the cupboard, in a shoe, or anywhere else that's not the toilet. What's more, because sleepwalking behaviors take place without conscious awareness, originating in the brain's central pattern generator where neural pathways for heavily practiced movements are stored, the perpetrator will have no recollection of the indiscretion.

## DOES WATCHING TOO MUCH TELEVISION RUIN YOUR EYESIGHT?

It's yet another warning that kids regularly hear from their parents: "Turn that TV off. Too much television is bad for your eyes." Well, is it?

No, not really. Not permanently, anyway.

Most experts agree that staring at the television won't cause any permanent damage to a person's eyes. Neither will staring at a computer screen or reading a lot of books. However, focusing your eyes for too long on any one thing can cause eye strain, a temporary problem.

The longer you focus on something, particularly without looking away to give your eyes a rest, the harder your eye muscles must work to maintain that focus. It makes your eye muscles fatigued and your eyes feel tired from too much use. Reading in dim light and even driving long distances can also contribute to eye strain.

Given that eye strain is just a temporary irritation, where did the myth of ruining your eyesight by watching too much television come from? It began in the 1960s when General Electric (GE) disclosed that many of their color televisions were faulty and emitting excessive X-rays.

GE rectified the problem by shielding the inner television tubes with leaded glass, but this wasn't before health officials warned of the harmful effects of the televisions, especially for children who sat too close and watched too much. This threat remained in the public consciousness, and the myth has continued to this day.

Now you can safely watch as much television as you like, and all you'll get is temporary eye strain resulting in tired, sore, dry eyes that will be back to normal after resting them.

## WHY DO MUSCLES SOMETIMES TWITCH?

Muscle twitching, also known as muscle fasciculation, involves small contractions in various muscles in the body, particularly the limbs, eyelids, and fingers. The contractions are involuntary and seem to come at the strangest times when you're least expecting them. What causes them?

While not a great deal of research has been done on the topic, it is thought that twitching muscles are caused by an irritation in the motor nerve that carries information from the brain to the muscle fibers. For some unknown reason, the axon of the nerve cells, which is the part that delivers the electrical signal to the muscle, can become hypersensitive to the electrical messages firing within it. When this happens, a signaling substance called acetylcholine is delivered to the muscle. Acetylcholine is an organic chemical that functions in the brain as a neurotransmitter to send signals to the muscles' cells, and it is these signals that results in the twitch.

Light, involuntary muscle twitches are very common and tend to occur after exercise or when people are stressed, tired, or lacking in nutrients. Caffeine and certain drugs can also cause them. And while they're still not well understood, muscle twitches don't cause any serious problems and can just be an irritation in themselves.

## WHAT IS THE LEGEND OF CASANOVA?

Giacomo Girolamo Casanova was an Italian adventurer who lived from 1725 to 1798. The legend of Casanova was large during his life and has only grown in the past two hundred years. A mere mention of his name evokes images of intrigue, adventure, and of course, seduction. His reputation with women has made his name synonymous with "womanizer." But there have been plenty of ladies' men throughout history. What made Casanova so special?

Casanova was much more than a womanizer. He was a scammer, an alchemist, a spy, a church cleric, an author, a dueler, a prisoner, and an escapee.

Born in Venice in 1725, Casanova was a brilliant child, entering the University of Padua at the age of twelve. Upon graduating, he took up the vices that would make him famous. He worked as a church cleric, but he gambled heavily, and his debts landed him in prison. After being released, he joined the military, but bored with being a soldier, he quit after a short while and left for Parma. He became a Freemason, wrote a play, and then, in 1753, after a grand tour in which he seduced dozens of women, returned to Venice.

However, the news of Casanova's escapades, including his romantic affairs with married women, nuns, and virgins, as well as his incessant gambling, finally caught up with him, and at age thirty, he was arrested by the Venice tribunal. He was sentenced to five years imprisonment for "public outrages against the holy religion." His cell, known as The Leads because of the lead plates covering the roof, was thought to be completely inescapable, but with the help of a priest in the cell above, Casanova escaped after thirteen months and fled to Paris. There he became an alchemist and was recruited as a spy, which brought him great wealth selling state bonds in Amsterdam. But he lost his money, went on the run again, and after eighteen years in exile, returned to Venice in 1774. Nine years later, after writing a vicious satire on the Venetian nobility, he was expelled again before being seized by Napoleon Bonaparte in 1797. He died one year later at the age of seventy-three.

Despite leading such a colorful life, Casanova is known today for his sexual conquests, which number more than two hundred. They, too, were more than checkered. He was accused of rape, contracted numerous diseases, and allegedly fathered his own grandson with his daughter Leonilda. He also deflowered many virgins, convincing them of his undying love before deserting them brokenhearted.

And the secret to his success in seducing women? Perhaps it was his famous wit, his charm, or his style (he powdered, scented, and curled his hair), but women adored him. In her 2006 book *Casanova's Women*, Judith Summers wrote: "As well as good looks, he possesses the rare gift of befriending women. He has the knack of addressing them as if they were his equals, and undressing them as if they were his superiors." He was the first celebrated ladies' man, is still the most famous, and men have been trying to emulate him ever since.

 ## HOW DID WOLVES BECOME DOGS?

As weird as it may seem, your cute and cuddly little poodle is descended from a line of vicious and bloodthirsty wolves. While wolves are dangerous predators, dogs are man's best friend. How did this dramatic change come about?

All dogs are descendants of ancient wolves. Fossils from Europe and Asia indicate that wolves were domesticated in these two different regions independently. But why did humans associate with ancient wolves at all?

1. **Hunting companions.** Scavenging wolves may have followed human hunting parties to take advantage of

the remains of carcasses. This may have led to wolves helping bring down injured prey in cooperative hunting techniques that benefitted both humans and wolves, leading to a closer association, and then domestication.

2. **Captured pups.** Humans may have captured wolf pups to deliberately bond with them for companionship and protection. Wolves are intelligent, social animals, and would have incorporated into a group of humans, eventually becoming domesticated.

3. **Taming adults.** If wolves were scavenging around human settlements, they may have been tamed and domesticated as they became more accustomed to the presence and benefits of humans.

As populations of wolves became domesticated, they began eating the foods people subsisted on—wheat, barley, corn, rice, and potatoes—and so evolved a set of genes that helped them to break down carbohydrates and starches. Then, as groups of wolves existed in isolation with people, they began to inbreed, resulting in genetic peculiarities. Where these peculiarities were found to have some function of  utility, personality, or beauty that humans found desirable, they would have been kept and promoted, maintaining them in the gene pool to produce a certain breed of dog.

Over thousands of years of selective breeding, around 300 unique breeds of dogs now exist today. Some are big, some are small, some are fast, some are strong. But they were all once wolves.

## ❓ DOES LISTENING TO MOZART REALLY MAKE BABIES SMARTER?

During a woman's pregnancy, you should play one of Mozart's symphonies loudly enough for the unborn baby to hear it, or better still, place some headphones on the mother's stomach. Known as the Mozart Effect, it is a well-known idea that playing classical musical to an unborn child will make them smarter. But is there any science to back up this suggestion?

French researcher Dr. Alfred A. Tomatisin first described the Mozart Effect in his 1991 book, *Pourquoi Mozart?* In it, he explored thirty years of research on the music of Mozart's ability to help mentally disabled children. Then, in 1993, a paper published in the journal *Nature* detailed an experiment where thirty-six college students were asked to undertake several spatial reasoning tasks. The students who had listened to ten minutes of Mozart beforehand performed better than those who hadn't. While the study only showed an increase in spatial intelligence, the results were popularly interpreted as an increase in overall IQ. This misconception, as well as the fact that Mozart was the only music listened to in the study, led to the association of his music with intelligence. The Mozart Effect was then widely reported, and a 1994 *New York Times* article by music columnist Alex Ross specifically stated that "listening to Mozart actually makes you smarter."

That's how it started, but is it true? Don Campbell, who has written more than twenty books on music, health, and  education, believes that music has a tremendous organizing quality for the brain and can modulate moods, as well as alleviate stress. "I know it improves our ability to be intelligent," he has said. However, psychologist Christopher Chabris of Union College in Schenectady, New York, performed a meta-analysis of sixteen studies related to the Mozart Effect in 1999. He found that listening to Mozart only slightly improved people's spatial skills and nothing else. Further, there is no evidence that classical music played to babies, pre- or post-natal, increases their intelligence or helps with cognitive abilities in any way.

Apart from the lack of evidence, critics cite that if parents are playing classical music to their babies and these babies turn out to be intelligent, it's probably more related to the fact that parents who listen to classical music are more likely to be intelligent themselves, and so produce smarter babies.

So, if you like Mozart's music, by all means keep listening to it, but don't expect it to turn your baby into a genius.

## HOW DOES BOUNTY HUNTING WORK?

$25,000 REWARD

DEAD OR ALIVE

TWENTY-FIVE THOUSAND DOLLARS will be paid by the City of New York for information leading to the capture of "LEPKE" BUCHALTER, aliases LOUIS BUCHALTER, LOUIS BUCKHOUSE, LOUIS KAWAR, LOUIS KAUVAR, LOUIS COHEN, LOUIS SAFFER, LOUIS BRODSKY.

WANTED FOR CONSPIRACY AND EXTORTION

LEWIS J. VALENTINE, Police Commissioner

In the Wild West, when outlaws like Jesse James roamed the plains and pillaged the towns, local sheriffs didn't have the manpower to track them down. "Wanted Dead or Alive" posters would be pinned up around town, offering huge rewards for the capture of these criminals. Jesse James was worth $5,000, and money like that attracted the toughest men in the country. Known as bounty hunters, these men would work tirelessly until they got their man, brought him to justice, and collected the reward. In modern times, the concept still exists, although the "Dead or Alive" part has been removed from the posters. Exactly how does bounty hunting work today?

A lot of times when a person is arrested, the court sets bail, which is an amount of money that person has to pay to stay out of jail until their court hearing. The bail money ensures they turn up for trial, because if they don't, the money is not refunded. Sometimes people can't afford to pay the bail, so a bail bondsman will provide a bail bond (which may be hundreds of thousands of dollars) from an insurance company. But if the accused skips town and misses the court appearance, the bail bondsman must pay the bail bond to the insurance company. Bail bondsmen are very reluctant to do this, and that's where the bounty hunter comes in.

Officially known as bail enforcement agents, the bounty hunter will track down the fugitive and bring him or her to justice so the bail is not forfeited. To do this, they generally research their subjects thoroughly, searching databases of addresses, phone numbers, license plate numbers, and social security numbers. They will stake out the fugitive's last known address and frequent haunts, and even employ surveillance cameras and night vision goggles. Much like a private investigator looking for a missing person, they will talk to friends and associates, doing whatever they can to track the person down. Bounty hunting can be a dangerous business, and many of these professionals carry guns and other weapons.

It is generally believed that bounty hunters are more effective than police, and, according to the National Association of Fugitive Recovery Agents (NAFRA), successfully apprehend nearly ninety percent of all bail jumpers. In return for their services, they typically receive somewhere between ten and twenty percent of the total bail bond.

But is this vigilante style of justice legal? The practice is illegal in most countries and is found almost exclusively in the United States and the Philippines. In the US, the NAFRA is the professional association representing the industry, which is generally legal. When the accused signs the bail bond contract, they agree that they can be arrested by the bail bond agent. All the bounty hunter needs is that piece of paper and an arrest can be made. The bail bond contract also gives the bounty hunter the right to enter the home of the fugitive to make the arrest. The laws do vary from state to state, however. Some states require bounty hunters to be licensed, while a number of states, including Illinois, Kentucky, Oregon, and Wisconsin prohibit the practice. Bounty hunters are, however, restricted to the United States and cannot operate across international borders.

Just as it was in the Wild West, bounty hunting today is a lucrative business and an integral part of the American justice system. The only real differences are: 1. There are more regulations and restrictions; 2. The fugitives can't be shot dead; and 3. There are reality TV shows about it, such as *Dog the Bounty Hunter*, that we get to watch over and over.

## DO HOUSEFLIES ONLY LIVE FOR 24 HOURS?

"I only got 24 hours to live, and I ain't gonna waste it here!" groans the disgruntled housefly in the 1998 animated film *A Bug's Life*. But do houseflies really have to cram their whole life into one day, or do they live longer than that?

Contrary to popular belief, the common fly (*Musca domestica*) lives much longer than 24 hours. All flies undergo a four-stage life cycle that consists of egg, larva, pupa, and adult stages. Females lay eggs that quickly hatch into larvae, also known as maggots. These worm-like maggots grow until they enter the pupal phase, when they grow hardened outer shells. During this time they grow legs and wings before a fully-grown fly emerges. An individual goes from maggot to adult in seven to ten days.

The adult fly usually lives for about two to three weeks. And as long as they don't meet with the business end of a fly swatter, flies in warmer temperatures can live for up to two months. The ideal temperature for a fly's survival is actually between 75 and 80 degrees—the temperature found in most American homes.

## IS IT DANGEROUS TO BE IN A SWIMMING POOL DURING A THUNDERSTORM?

If you're swimming in a pool and a thunderstorm starts building, the first thing you'll see is people getting out of the water, and the first thing you'll hear, apart from the thunder, is the panic-stricken warnings from people to get out of the water immediately. Should these warnings be heeded, or are you okay to swim on?

Heed the warnings.

Lightning is random and unpredictable. An electrical discharge always seeks out the shortest path to the ground. The shortest path not only refers to the physical distance, but also to the level of resistance. If there's something more conductive in the vicinity of the highest point, the lightning may hit that instead. Since water is an excellent conductor of electricity, this is often a body of water.

For a number of reasons, it's dangerous to be in a swimming pool if lightning is around. Because the water is a good conductor, it will attract the lightning. But for you to be in danger, the lightning doesn't actually have to strike you directly. If it strikes the water near to you, the current may still give you a fatal shock. Swimming pools are also connected to a much larger surface area via underground water pipes and electric wiring for filters and lights. If the lightning strikes the ground anywhere along this conductive network, it could produce a shock in the pool itself.

Swimmers do, in fact, get struck by lightning. In 2005, three people were struck while swimming in the ocean near Tampa, and four more were struck in waters off Chiba Prefecture, Japan. Then, in 2006, a fifty-year-old British man was dangling his feet in a swimming pool at a rented villa in Italy when lightning struck the water, killing him and injuring his friend. Fish in open waters also get killed, but as most of the lightning current flows across the surface of the water, many fish that swim deeper remain unaffected.

The National Lightning Safety Institute recommends a very conservative approach toward swimming during a thunderstorm. Any time you hear thunder you should immediately get out of the water and into a safe place. And all pool activities should be suspended until at least thirty minutes after the last clap of thunder is heard. The upshot— swimming during a thunderstorm is one of the most dangerous things you can do.

## WHO OWNS WALL GRAFFITI?

Many graffiti artists and their original works have become iconic. The British artist Banksy, who painted the boy with the words "I remember when all this was trees" on a wall in Detroit's Packard Plant, is just one example. Some of these people are clearly talented artists, and yet their work is affixed to private property, often without permission. Who owns the graffiti, and do the artists themselves have any right to restrict the subsequent exploitation of their works?

The owner of the property owns the medium upon which the graffiti is placed, and so will own the physical original of the work. If graffiti is on a wall, the owner of that wall can

physically do what they wish with it, such as removing it or painting over it. The graffiti artist will generally have no recourse if their work is destroyed.

Then there is the issue of the copyright in the graffiti. Under US copyright law, an artist owns the exclusive rights of a creative work, and these rights can only be forfeited through an act of licensing or transferring that right to another person. This means that the artist has control over the reproduction and distribution of copies of the work, and may receive damages if these rights are violated. There are, however, conflicting views as to whether the underlying illegality of graffiti precludes the protection of copyright. The 2002 US case of Villa v. Brady Publishing commented that graffiti was likely copyrightable, and there is a strong argument that simply because a piece of art was created as vandalism does not alter the artist's copyright in that work.

But there's a catch-22 when it comes to the graffiti artists enforcing their rights for any breach of copyright. If, for example, somebody reproduces and sells the artwork, to assert their rights, the graffiti artist would need to claim ownership of the copyright, thereby admitting to the crime of vandalism. This could lead to criminal prosecution or to a tortious lawsuit for trespass. In addition, many graffiti artists cultivate an aura of secrecy around their work, and bringing a legal claim would result in a potentially undesirable public unmasking.

There have been a number of cases of graffiti artists seeking recourse when others have profited from their works, but the issue has not been finally resolved. In 2011, an out-of-court settlement was reached by a group of street artists who sued Fiat for using their art without permission in an advertisement. Stacey Richman, the lawyer who represented the artists, said: "These people are generally living hand to mouth, and if the corporations are going to take advantage of their work, they deserve to be paid." But until there is a superior court case to decide the issue definitively, the rights of graffiti artists will remain a gray area, just like the walls they paint on.

## ❔ WHY DOES SEEING FOOD MAKE YOUR MOUTH WATER?

Picture a tender, juicy steak accompanied by salty fries straight out of the oven. Or a rich piece of chocolate cake with thick icing. Is your mouth watering yet? What causes our mouths to water whenever we see or smell, or even think of, delicious food?

Saliva plays an important role in eating and digestion. It lubricates the food we eat, helping us to work it around in our mouths for chewing. It also contains enzymes that start the digestion process. These enzymes help break down the food in the mouth, before it even reaches the stomach.

When we see or smell delicious food, the brain processes these senses, sending a signal to the salivary glands to produce the saliva in preparation for eating. The brain anticipates the fact that the food will be eaten, and as a reflex action, produces saliva in advance, allowing us to eat immediately. This would have been particularly important for our ancestors, who might have had to eat quickly after

making a kill before scavenging predators arrived on the scene.

In fact, one of the enzymes in our saliva is called salivary amylase, which breaks down starches. Humans carry extra copies of the gene that encodes this enzyme, and scientists believe this may have helped to hasten human evolution. Humans carry as many as fifteen copies of the gene, compared to chimpanzees, who only have two. We probably developed more to deal with a changing diet in early humans that may have fueled an increase in the size of human brains and bodies.

The phrase "mouth-watering" is actually very accurate. There are two types of saliva, mucous and serous. Mucous saliva is thick and sticky, while serous saliva is very watery. It is this serous saliva that floods your mouth at the smell or sight of particularly ambrosial food.

## IF A TREE FALLS IN A FOREST, DOES IT MAKE A SOUND?

This is a philosophical thought experiment regarding observation and the knowledge of reality: If a tree falls in a forest and no one is around to hear it, does it make a sound?

This conundrum has been posed for hundreds of years. In *A Treatise Concerning the Principles of Human Knowledge*, published in 1710, Irish philosopher George Berkeley first discussed the concept that trees in a garden are there no longer than while there is somebody to perceive them. Then, in 1883, an article in *The Chautauquan* asked: "If a tree were to fall on an island where there were no human beings, would there be any sounds?" The article went on to answer the question with: "No. Sound is the sensation excited in the ear when the air or other medium is set in motion." The current phrasing of the question originated in the 1910 book *Physics*, written by Charles Riborg Mann and George Ransom Twiss.

To answer the question, here are the philosophical and the physiological perspectives.

## Metaphysics—The Philosophical View

As with many issues in philosophy, a number of questions are posed.

Can something exist outside of human perception? This argument proposes that if nobody is around to see, hear, touch, or smell a tree, it cannot be said to exist, because what is to say it exists when such an existence is unknown?

Can we assume that the unobserved world functions in the same way as the observed world? While many scientists claim that the presence of an observer doesn't change whether a falling tree makes a sound or not, this is an impossible claim to prove.

What is the difference between what something is and how it appears? If a tree exists outside our perception, then it will produce sound waves when it falls, but these sound waves will not actually *sound* like anything. Sound as it is mechanically understood will occur, but sound as it is understood by human sensation will not occur.

## Physics—The Physiological View

From a scientific viewpoint, the tree and the sound exist regardless of whether they are being observed. Sound is a hearable noise, and the tree will make a sound even if nobody hears it. Sound is produced by a mechanical wave of pressure and displacement through a medium such as air or water. We don't have to perceive a sound to know that the laws of physics apply. The sound that a tree makes is defined by these laws, and the auditory sensation as it is perceived is secondary. In physics, sound is not dependent upon perception, so a tree will make a sound when it falls, regardless of who is around to perceive it.

So what's the answer? It depends on how the concept of sound is interpreted. If we look at sound physically, the tree does make a sound in all situations, but if we look at sound as our ability to perceive it, then the tree only makes a sound if somebody is there to hear it. Either way, the question is impossible to either prove or disprove, which is what has made it such an enduring riddle.

# Artwork Credits

Images are from shutterstock.com unless otherwise noted.

Front cover: fan © Philip
Anthony; cheese © Sketch
Master; rabbit © silver tiger;
bison © andrey oleynik;
dinosaur © alongzo; eye ©
Hein Nouwens; insect ©
Artur Balytskyi; hat © alex74;
spider © Artur Balytskyi;
samurai © Canicula; lizard ©
KUCO

Back cover: whip ©
danilobiancalana; cat © Tony
Campbell; crying woman ©
Ljupco Smokovski; zebra ©
prapass; grave © Mega Pixel

p. 1: © aerogondo2
p. 5: © iGuide
p. 7: © Ten03
p. 9: © omnimoney
p. 11: © Lapina
p. 14: © Dean Drobot
p. 16: © Ghost Bear (bison)
and © Thanakorn Hongphan
(buffalo)
p. 18: © Raisa Kanareva
p. 20: © Sergiy Kuzmin
p. 23: © AlinaMD
p. 25: © Delmas Lehman
p. 28: © Dmitrijs Bindemanis
p. 30: © Richard Peterson
p. 33: © sarahkvech
p. 35: © nullplus

p. 36: © XiXinXing
p. 39: © ALEKSEI SEMYKIN
p. 41: © focuslight
p. 43: © DUSAN ZIDAR
p. 44: © Nejron Photo
p. 46: © ArtOfPhotos
p. 49: © Rob Byron
p. 50: © Lolostock
p. 52: © Cora Reed
p. 55: © Zastolskiy Victor
p. 57: © GUDKOV ANDREY
p. 59: © swa182
p. 60: © tommaso79
p. 62: © Andrey_Popov
p. 66: © TunedIn by Westend61
p. 68: © cagi
p. 70: © Igor Brisker
p. 72: © Richard Goldberg
p. 75: © Vaclav Volrab
p. 77: © gresei
p. 79: © Super Prin
p. 82: © evp82
p. 85: © Laura Gangi Pond
p. 86: © Maya Kruchankova
p. 91: © simongee
p. 93: © aslysun
p. 95: © Yellow Cat
p. 97: © "Shoeless" Joe Jackson
and Kenesaw Mountain
Landis courtesy of the Library
of Congress
p. 99: © Rainer Plendl

# About the Author

**Andrew Thompson** divides his time between Australia and England. A lawyer by trade, his obsession with finding out the truth about aspects of the world that we take for granted has led him to accumulate a vast body of knowledge, which he has distilled into book form. He is the author of the four Ulysses Press bestsellers *What Did We Use Before Toilet Paper?*, *Can Holding in a Fart Kill You?*, *Why Do Roller Coasters Make You Puke?*, and *Hair of the Dog to Paint the Town Red*. See all of Andrew's books at www.andrewthompsonwriter.co.uk or at Twitter @AndrewTWriter.